Killers Are Fatherless

The Real Cause Of School Shootings, Serial Killings, And Gang Murders

L. Salvatore Scarpitta

KILLERS ARE FATHERLESS

THE REAL CAUSE OF SCHOOL SHOOTINGS, SERIAL KILLINGS, AND GANG MURDERS

by L. Salvatore Scarpitta

Multi-Services Publishing:
info@multiservicespublishing.com

**PLEASE REPORT INSTANCES OF CONTENT THAT
MAY HAVE BEEN STOLEN OR PLAGIARIZED
FROM THIS BOOK.**

Contact us at:
stolencontent@killersarefatherless.com
Or try the website at:
KillersAreFatherless.com
...or notify the publisher.
As with all technology, websites and emails may not always be
available.

Killers Are Fatherless

The Real Cause Of School Shootings, Serial Killings, And Gang Murders

Multi-Services Publishing

multiservicespublishing.com

SINCE 1989

Available in paperback, ebook, and audiobook formats.

Contents

About the Author

So you'll know who's talking to you, here's a small bit about the author.

The author spent nearly 30 years at many levels of education as both a teacher and administrator. He holds a Bachelor of Arts degree in Psychology from the California State University system. He also holds a Master of Arts degree in Educational Administration. He attended a variety of other colleges and universities, including in the University of California system.

The author has held multiple teaching certifications in two states. Credentialed subject matter areas have included: Mathematics, Multiple Subjects (generally used for elementary teaching, but also for general subject, self-contained high schools or adult classes), Social Studies (including U.S. History and U.S. Government), Business Education, ESL (English as a Second Language), and Psychology. He has also taught a variety of other subjects. Additionally, he was a certificated teacher at the community college level.

He has held an Administrative Credential in a second state which included certifications for Principal, Administration, and Curriculum.

He has taught multiple subjects at several grade levels in two states. He also worked as an administrator, including as principal.

Previously, he held a California Private Post-Secondary Certificate of Authorization for Service authorizing teaching Writing (English) and Mathematics in California private post-secondary schools (vocational schools for adults).

Beyond education, the author has had broad life experience in many other areas of life. As part of that, the author spent a number of years in both the U.S. Army (enlisted) and the U.S. Navy as a commissioned officer.

Also see the related book, *Education Is Dead: Reflections on a Failed Public Education System* also by the author.

For more information about the author, see the *About The Author* sections in the book, *The Cartainos: Men of Passion • Men of Stone.*

PREFACE

Several sections of this book are reprinted, adapted, or abridged directly from the 2022 book, *The Cartainos: Men of Passion • Men of Stone*, which I wrote over a 12-year period. As I originally researched and wrote those sections in their different context, I could not help but feel that that research and accompanying insights had a meaning well beyond its focus in *The Cartainos*. That was especially true as I looked at much of the continuing violence throughout America — and the world.

Although those several sections are taken from *The Cartainos*, do not misunderstand the family talked about in that book. As a disclaimer, the violence the book in your hands discusses was not present in the Cartaino family. However, the issue of fatherlessness affected that family, nonetheless, as it has in countless other families.

I felt it wise to put those insights and writings into this different context so that it might move people to understand the absolutely critical importance of good fathers present in the lives of their children and of healthy families, generally.

I'll mention here that, regardless of my degrees and certifications, I am neither a doctor nor a mental health professional. I'm an observer with broad life experience. Take the observations and suggestions in this book in that light.

This is not a book on parenting. It is here for one thing only: to call out one seemingly obvious commonality among the vast majority of killers.

The focus of this book is on the issue of fatherlessness, rather than specifically on dysfunctional families. However, in many cases, one can certainly lead to the other. In what appears to be a large majority of cases, dysfunctional families are indeed often related to issues of bad or absent fathers. That might seem to be obvious.

I'll add upfront that, even in the absence of fathers, good and strong mothers can do much to reduce the damage of a missing or bad father. In other cases, truly terrible mothers are themselves the problem in families. One particularly egregious example of that is discussed in *The Cartainos*.

There is plenty of data on the damage caused by absent fathers. Data is not the same regarding mothers. Therefore, because this book is about fatherlessness, we will not specifically discuss mothers. However, nothing is straightforward. Neither the data nor the observations and comments found in this book apply in every case or to every family. But they do apply so often that the observations, warnings, and suggestions you'll find here should be taken seriously.

I'll also say, and repeat throughout the book, that just because a child is raised without a father, does not mean that child will become a bad or violent person. In fact, there are *many* who become truly wonderful people. Some are recognized as such throughout the world. Others become heroes. In no way is this an attack on the countless people who grew up fatherless.

However, fatherlessness and dysfunctional families are seen so often among so many of the most violent, some would say evil killers, that this should no longer be ignored. Too often, it is mentioned in passing before moving on to those issues which are not at all the foundation of violence and evil.

Many statistics, some older, some newer, are quoted in the sections adapted from *The Cartainos*. That information has been around for many, many years, yet little or nothing of substance has been done, other than by individuals and small organizations. Even then, results have been limited. I strongly feel that the facts of fatherlessness speak for themselves. Further, the problem has not changed except, perhaps, to worsen. Therefore, old statistics and conclusions are effectively as valid today as newer research in more recent times. The problem and its effects continue to wreak havoc.

There comes a point when one would think it can no longer be ignored. Yet it is. It is swept away. It is passed over quickly, sometimes barely acknowledging it at all.

Why is that?

It's often because it's so difficult to get measurable understandings of what goes on in the secrecy and hidden lives of most families. Sometimes, assumptions might be made based on just small tidbits of information about a father or family. But accuracy is often very difficult when looking into the private lives of families. Nonetheless, we have plenty of information to raise the same red flags which have been raised for many, many years, but have been largely ignored.

It's likely this issue is so often passed over, or just briefly mentioned, because no one knows what to do about it. Some people are in denial about it regardless of the ever-present statistics and corroborating facts of real people's lives — and deaths.

Therefore, it is often mentioned, though just in passing, and then ignored.

It won't be ignored here.

Chapter 1

Defining The Word

Before beginning, let me clarify — once again — that this book is about killers. It is not simply about fatherless children. The book's title is "KILLERS Are Fatherless." The corollary is not necessarily true at all. Children who are fatherless are NOT necessarily killers. There are many wonderful fatherless children in the world. But I stand by the title of this book: In the vast number of cases, killers are indeed fatherless.

***

People talk past each other about fatherlessness because they each define "fatherlessness" differently. I'll start by defining its use in this book and frequently distinguish it with how others too often define it.

Webster's Third New International Dictionary, Unabridged (1993), includes, among others, this definition for father (which includes fathering): *"to care for and look after as a father might."* Although that meaning was more commonly used years ago, it remains valid today and is how many continue to use it — including in this book.

Of course, one is left to ask, "Okay. But how does a father look after his children?" There is a built-in assumption that this means *good* care and *good* looking after. After all, that is what a *good* father does. So, is Merriam-Webster's definition missing that one critical word?

To be "fatherless" is to be without being looked after or being cared for as a father might — sensibly understood to be an actual father, generally a good one. That's how this book uses it. A good and effective father *stand-in,* often a stepfather, might be able to provide that care, too.

However, for many years, data has appeared to show that stepfathers are problematic more often than are biological fathers. Whenever possible, an actual, hopefully *biological* father is best.

Those who object and deny that killers are often linked to fatherlessness are those who are most inclined to define "father" so narrowly as to eliminate any other definition for it. Therefore, if a father is home with his children, they are not "fatherless" even if that father sits all day drinking beer, deriding his wife and children, and complaining about life.

Such people insist that such children are not fatherless at all. They say that, even though such men do nothing to provide *any* fathering at all for their children, let alone *good* fathering, those children are not fatherless. Yet even children with such fathers often support the perspective by deniers that they are not fatherless at all. That's true from a biological perspective — but nothing more.

Frankly — and to make things clearer to some of the conceptually-confused — children actually suffer from a lack of *good* fathering. We might use a new word for that: *fatheringlessness.* But that really seems unnecessarily convoluted.

So here, together with others, we generally just say fatherlessness and we know what it means and what it includes.

Perhaps we should really say *"a lack of good fathering"* every time. That would make all of this more understandable to those who insist on taking the term "fatherless" too literally.

Nonetheless, so that we can be clear to those who might still be confused, I'll repeat that, when we talk about "fatherlessness" in this book, we actually mean *"a lack of (good) fathering."* Others may insist "fatherlessness" only and always means the physical absence of a father *of any sort.* But it's certainly unwise to accept that.

Additionally, I will not be addressing specific concerns about the "breakdown of the nuclear family." While that is absolutely a valid concern, it's actually misleading.

The damage from fatherlessness has been happening for centuries, even millennia. When people refer to the issue of family breakdown, it is often presented as though it is a more recent concern. Some speak as though all had been good with fathers and families prior to perhaps 60 or 70 years ago — maybe even less.

Yes, some aspects of the family were indeed better back then, especially related to stronger standards of a shared morality. However, even then, fatherlessness negatively affected children. Even back then, and much before, the world saw that some of the world's worst killers were fatherless sons.

As I'll consistently say, fatherlessness does not mean children will become violent as they become older children and then adults. In most cases, they certainly won't. However, those children who *do* become killers of multiple people, even as adults, were frequently fatherless. That's an important distinction.

Of course, things are always more complicated than this, but that understanding and use of the word will be the focus of this book.

Specifically, here is how fatherlessness will be defined in this book. You'll see it again, sometimes shorter or with slightly different nuances.

Children are "fatherless" if a good — generally biological — father had not been present to provide good fathering for his children during effectively all the years when they were growing to adulthood. Actual ages at what might appropriately be considered adulthood vary. Children with fathers technically present, but who provide no or low-quality fathering, are still growing up without a functioning father. They are still fatherless.

Others may use looser, more general definitions in order to suggest that fatherlessness is not really the foundational problem that it is. However, in studying commonly shared traits among killers, that definition is consistent among almost all of them.

Chapter 2

Categories And Historical Examples Of Killers

There are two things in this chapter. First, we'll define in general terms the categories of killers considered in this book. Second, we'll list some examples.

CATEGORIES

Wars are clearly mass killing events. That is a separate issue. Here, we consider events of multiple deaths for whom responsibility can generally be laid on one or two individuals. Elsewhere, it may be different but, for our purpose here, there are five categories of those taking the lives of others on a large scale.

(1) Authoritarian Dictators and Despots.

Under this category, we see the largest number of deaths, many times into the millions. Although guns have certainly been used, especially in more recent times, guns have not been used in the greatest numbers of deaths over the centuries. Vast numbers of deaths have been inflicted by starvation, torture, deaths in labor camps, burning, and by other means. Most infamously, gas chambers and ovens were used by Germany to kill millions during the Holocaust in World War II.

(2) Serial Killers.

Serial killers are often not remembered since they often work less dramatically. They may kill their victims one or two at a time. One definition suggests defining one who causes the deaths of three or more people in separate events as a serial killer. But, in total, serial killers can kill far more than that. Victims of multiple serial killers have numbered in the hundreds.

Even among serial killers who have fewer victims, deaths often far exceed what people see today even among some of the most deadly school shooters. Although guns have been used, they have not generally been the choice of weapon for most serial killers. Personal strangulation is common, but knives and other means of death are also used.

(3) Mass Killers (not at schools).

This category is sometimes defined as events in which four or more people are killed in one killing event. For our purposes here, that definition's base figure may be too low. There are other factors — not merely the numbers — that go into defining something as a mass killing. For now, I leave this undefined.

Although guns are often used by these killers, they are not used exclusively. Certainly, this category includes mass shooters, but bombs, knives, and even vehicular killings of people in open crowds are also employed. These are often dramatic and newsworthy. Some are identified as terrorist killings. In other cases, numbers can include dozens of deaths and more. In other cases, as in the terrorist killings on 9/11, numbers can be in the thousands. Note that planes were the weapons of choice for those terrorists.

. . .

(4) School Shooters.

This is the category that appears to trouble people the most, even though far more children have been killed in the previous categories. We all want to feel that schools are safe for children — and for all of us. Here, guns are widely used by students to kill other students, teachers, and staff. People feel these situations are especially heinous because innocent children are slaughtered. We are disturbed not just because the victims are often young children, but that the killers themselves are children. In the overall picture, only school shooters seem to demand such widespread and ongoing attention.

(5) "Common" Murderers.

This category includes other killings throughout the country. These killings are so common that they often just warrant brief mentions in the daily news. Yet, taken altogether, these killers take many, many lives — tens of thousands in a single year. For example, FBI statistics estimate that, in 2020, approximately 20,000 homicides occurred in the U.S.[1] However, because many jurisdictions don't report crime numbers to the FBI, that number is undoubtedly too low.

Included in many of these killings are gang activities. Those killers not only kill other gang members, but also many innocents not in gangs. Also in this category are "general" criminals, including those with and without mental illnesses. A large majority of killings in this category involve guns.

Especially when including deaths at the hands of political despots, guns have not been implicated in the majority of deaths mentioned above. However, getting rid of guns, even if possible, would not even stop the countless other killings mentioned above. As is seen elsewhere, killers will find other ways to kill. Therefore, guns are not the root cause of violence. We will look at this issue again later on.

EXAMPLES/EVIDENCE

I'm aware that I'm referring to the coming examples as "evidence." Others would call all this mere supposition. After all, some say, objective researchers wouldn't accept this, calling its merely anecdotal. Some might also say that, even with the overwhelming numbers of killers who are "fatherless" — as defined in this book — there is not enough evidence that fatherlessness itself is a main cause of violence and that it provides an environment — or lack of environment — that allows some sons (far more sons than daughters) to become killers. But these examples are actually quite significant.

The infamy of those on the coming list is overwhelming. There are no other commonalities among them, of which we know, other than fatherlessness itself — and the lack of an effective foundation of morality, at least as has been accepted in more recent times.

Categories of weapons and methodologies of death are different among them. Mental illness does not appear to be present, independent of fatherlessness, among substantive enough numbers of those listed to identify it as a pervasive commonality. (However, mental illness *is* present more commonly among some killers — including among some school shooters.)

But these killers do share one thing: their upbringing meets the criteria of fatherlessness as defined in this book.

To think this list does not support the thesis of fatherlessness should be concerning. This has been seen for so many years in so many killers that, when we see damage so consistent and so pervasive, we must take this far more seriously than we've been doing. We will look at just some of the research on fatherlessness shortly.

If the magnitude of the fatherless individuals below does not shake people up, it's not likely they will be moved by anything.

People will continue to die while such people wait for yet more "studies" or hearings on it. That's just the sort of thing that ensures nothing will get done — and that more people will die — as has been happening for so many years.

As in education, but also in other areas, there is already more than enough research available on which to take immediate action. The price of further delays by demanding and then waiting interminably for yet more studies or hearings will be paid in the number of continuing deaths.

Those who might want to nit-pick the names below to show how one or another actually had a good father growing up aren't really looking at the full extent of this problem. It's certainly easy to debate one killer or another and thereby put off action on the entire crisis. That's exactly what's been happening for countless years now. It would be rare to find a naysayer who was intimately involved in the death of an innocent. None want further delays.

Let's look more closely at why we're able to confidently generalize that the vast numbers of killers share the single common foundational cause of fatherlessness (or dysfunctional families).

(1) An enormous number of gang members and others committing violence — primarily in the cities and primarily male — grow up with missing or low-quality fathers. Although sources on this can be quoted later, realistically, it's already widely known.

(2) In the case of serial killers, let's take a quick look at the those discussed in just a single book: *The Killer Book of Serial Killers* (2009), by Tom and Michael Philbin. This book contains chapters on more than 36 violent serial killers. Where information was missing on certain serial killers discussed in the book, some of that information was then found in *The Big Book of Serial Killers*, Volume 1 (2017) and Volume 2 (2019), by Jack Rosewood and Rebecca Lo or in other sources.

Of those more than 36 serial killers, 28 had indications of being fatherless or being from a dysfunctional family. (At least one mentions a fully dysfunctional mother.) Another two leave open this possibility but lack information to make a definitive judgment on their likely fatherlessness.

Of this group of 28 to 30, it's possible that perhaps just *one* may not have had a dysfunctional father or family — and we're not fully sure about that one. The rest on the list make *no mention* of the situations with their fathers or families when they were children.

That is by no means an indication that they had healthy and involved fathers or families. Indeed, the pattern shows it is most likely that, as with the others, they, too, had dysfunctional fathers and families. I believe we are very likely to find that they suffered the same damage of fatherlessness which may have lead, in this case, to their becoming serial killers.

Is it a coincidence that nearly the entirety of those listed have one or more things (as mentioned in the books on serial killers) that identify them as likely having been raised with a bad or absent father or in a dysfunctional family? It's no coincidence at all.

(3) But it's this next list that is most powerfully revealing. Here we'll find many of the most infamous killers in world history. If anyone looks at this list — more are found in Chapter Seven — and insists that there is actually some *other* trait or cause commonly shared among these killers that might have led to the horrors they committed — guns, mental illness, bullying, or whatever — there may be little more that I or anyone can do to make the case to you for the damage of fatherlessness.

Remember that, for our purposes here, *Children are "fatherless" if a good — generally biological — father had not been present to provide good fathering for his children during all or nearly all the years when they were growing to adulthood. Actual ages at what might appropriately be considered adulthood vary. The mere physical presence of a poor or uninvolved father in the home can still leave children "fatherless."*

With that in mind, here are some of history's most infamous fatherless tyrants and killers — followed by some other fatherless killers:

Genghis Khan (circa 1162-1227), *Vladimir Lenin* (1870-1924), *Joseph Stalin* (1878-1953), *Adolf Hitler* (1889-1945), *Mao Zedong* (1893-1976), *Idi Amin* (1925-2003), *Saddam Hussein* (1937-2006), *Osama Bin Laden* (1957-2011).

To that list, I add these:

Charles Manson, Richard Speck, Ted Bundy, Stephen Paddock, Nikolas Cruz, Salvador Ramos.

What's critical here is that there are *countless* others. But those lists should shake anyone up as to the issue of fatherlessness.

We'll consider more detail for each name in that list, as well as others, in Chapter Seven, *"Fatherless Sons."*

---

1. *Some FBI crime statistics may be found at:*
   cde.ucr.cjis.gov/LATEST/webapp/#/pages/home, accessed 2-9-2023.

Chapter 3

Exactly What Is Fatherlessness?

As I'll repeat... "Children are "fatherless" if a good — generally biological — father had not been present to provide good fathering for his children during effectively all the years when they were growing to adulthood. Actual ages at what might be appropriately considered adulthood vary. Children with fathers technically present, but who provide no or low-quality fathering, are still growing up without a functioning father. They are still fatherless."

The problem with fatherlessness is not simply the increasing breakdown of the family, as some people think. Things have indeed become much worse. In large part, that is because of a significantly changed or discarded national moral foundation. However, we must be looking at the forest of this problem over the past centuries, not just its trees over more recent decades.

BEING A MAN

One serious problem is that not only do men not always know

how to be fathers, many don't know how to be men. Many have grown up without strong roll models in their own lives and, even when they want to, just don't know how to do it.

Morally strong and loving men are respected and emulated. Strength doesn't necessarily mean physical strength. It certainly does not mean an aggressive domination of others.

Children need roll models growing up. Their father should be one of their best. But a father can't and shouldn't be one who himself is a mess. Those who are can make a new start and become men respected not just by others, but by themselves.

Men who do the wrong things should not be looked upon as role models for their children, although in too many cases, they will be.

Those who abuse drugs, alcohol, or their families, who are actual criminals or who hang around undesirable men or gangs, are not positive roll models.

Fathers, ensure you are a good man. Be a role model that will allow your children to grow up as positive and happy human beings. Be such a man not only for your children, but for others, including your wife — if you are able to have one.

Join a church. Learn to believe in God and live accordingly. Find out what a good man really is. Read multiple books, not just on becoming a better father, but on becoming a better man, on manhood itself.

Join a positive organization of men — perhaps at a church — without significantly interfering with your duties as a father and husband. If you later find that organization or its members don't have the values they should have, leave it and find another.

If you need to, make a complete change in your life.

This doesn't apply to all men. Many are already fine men. But, in a world of fatherlessness, this must be said.

ANSWERING QUESTIONS

Let me answer some questions on this book's definition of

fatherlessness which we again read as this chapter began. Answers are repetitious because people wanting to discard or lower the importance of fathers are themselves repetitious.

(1) (Q) *Your definition of fatherlessness is very restrictive. Children can grow up with a father even if he isn't around until adulthood, even if he's not home all the time because he has to work. That's a ridiculous definition!*

(A) You're correct. It's indeed a tough and rigid definition. But this is the definition that fits those children and adults who later become violent. Less restrictive definitions will let increasing numbers of violent people slip through the cracks as other definitions leave out the full gamut of fathering. Fathering of older children is certainly different from fathering younger children. Good fathering is needed at all ages, until they reach full adulthood. That's not a legally-defined adulthood. It's *actual* adulthood and that can vary significantly among children.

Note that there have been a great many people who lost their fathers as older teens or as young adults. They are then affected by it throughout the entirety of their lives. The need for fathering does not expire. Here's a more succinct answer: The definition of fatherlessness in this book appears to provide the single commonality shared by what appear to be the vast majority of killers.

(2) (Q) *I have known plenty of out-of-control children who have their fathers living with them at home! Even growing up with a father has nothing to do with how children can turn out!*

(A) Again, you're absolutely correct. There are many such children with fathers at home. But here are the key and operative words in our definition of fatherless children: a GOOD father. It can't just be a male body coexisting with children in the same house. It must be an involved father providing good fathering. Yes, I know it's difficult. I can't help that. It's what children actually need. It's what the vast majority of killers didn't have.

A father is generally a good father if he is regularly and positively involved with his children as they grow, if he provides love, guidance, help, and life instruction — and if he regularly talks to them.

He — and their mother — also need to regularly monitor their children's lives to ensure he — and their mother — know what their children are doing. At times, that may involve appropriate corrections which are effective enough to deter a child from making wrong turns in life. These aren't hard and fast requirements. Results in adulthood will determine if a father had been successful but, by then, it will be too late if he was not successful. (A reminder, though, that this book is not about how to parent.)

(3) (Q) *You can't tell me that almost all, or even just a simple majority of violent people were fatherless according to your very restrictive definition! I can't believe that. Where is your evidence! How can you know what sort of parenting killers have had?*

(A) Actually, I *am* telling you that. But your point is a good one. How do we actually know about *anyone's* parenting? In many, even most cases, whether a person of violence was raised with good or bad parenting is difficult to assess. But enough pieces can be put together to make that generalization. As will be noted later, having an involved father or a healthy family is often judged in the press by the *lack* of certain things rather than by the presence of other things. For example, if there is no immediate evidence of abuse, poverty, marital discord, an absent father, or similar things, many choose to judge that there was nothing wrong in that child's upbringing.

But the *absence* of some easily observable bad things does not mean the *presence* of other critically important things. Often, fathers and parents self-report their own parenting. Many really bad fathers actually *do* report that they were not good fathers. They do that because they often regret not having been better. However, other fathers, and parents generally, self-report that they have been good parents — whether or not that was truly the case. That is really hard to know.

What children say can be helpful in that, but not always. Sometimes even children don't understand what's really been going on. Neighbors and even family friends may or may not have the full picture either. I have looked at these issues as closely as available resources allow. Judgments are then made.

(4) (Q) *Tell me how you or any of us are able to make judgments about this. I still don't really believe it's the problem you say it is.*

(A) Where family data exists concerning the upbringing of future killers, it almost always leans to the side of absent or low-quality fathering or dysfunctional families. It does it so often that it can not be ignored. There have indeed been cases of what, at least on the surface, *appear* to be good fathers and good families. But they are comparatively rare enough that we must move to champion the position taken in this book.

Statistics over many years — some of which will be quoted shortly — also back what I say here. You'll find it's far easier to find killer children (and adults) with hints of, or actual low-quality or missing fathers and dysfunctional families than it is to find the opposite among killers.

(5) (Q) *Regardless of what you say, I still don't believe that almost all killers were fatherless or from dysfunctional families! That's absurd.*

(A) Generally, I'd tell you to do a bit of your own research. Sadly, you'll find there are multiple ways to define fatherlessness out there, all far looser than what is in this book. Other simplistic definitions allow reporters and other authors to maintain that there aren't as many fatherless killers as actually exist.

***

Here is more about this concern:

One shooter was raised by his father through childhood and was, we are wrongly told, not fatherless. For our purposes here, it doesn't matter who the shooter was. What matters is the grossly deficient definition of being "raised by a father through childhood" and that, therefore, the child was not fatherless. Childhood often means a younger child, not necessarily an older teen nearly ready to leave home.

For anyone who has talked to people whose father died when they were still a teenager —16, 17, 18, 19, for example — especially daughters — one would absolutely know that damage had been done. Sometimes, it takes an outsider to objectively look at that older child — even a fully-grown one — to see the predictable character traits or life choices that are strongly tied to children who grow up without a father.

An older (or adult) child may not even be aware of that. Limiting judgment to some ill-defined time period of "childhood" is foolish. The loss of a father even well beyond childhood can have lifelong repercussions.

The next assumption, regularly made, is that if a child, a later killer, grew up throughout his childhood with a father at home, he was not fatherless. By itself, that can be an incorrect assumption. As repeatedly already said in this book, people know that a father can be physically home, but mentally and emotionally absent. The mere presence of a father at home does not make a child fathered. Having a father for purposes of avoiding later damage means having a good father who actually fathers his children.

Too many commentators insist that fatherlessness isn't the big deal people say it is. They call for yet "more studies." As in education, we've had plenty of substantive studies. Even without them, you don't have to be a university-trained researcher to look at the facts and not conclude that fatherlessness appears to have had a foundational impact on children. Is it a coincidence that a majority of killers were impacted by fathers who were weak, absent, or otherwise had a troubled relationship with their fathers?

Refusing to accept what is now obvious to many, one commentator says this:

> "It is clear to me that there needs to be more research on mass shooters before any link between fatherlessness can be established. What we do know is that *fatherlessness is something that increases the odds of criminal behavior* overall." [Emphasis added.]

Later, that same article adds:

> "...a growing body of evidence shows a high correlation between fatherlessness and violence among young men..."

So let me understand this. The article acknowledges:
(1) Fatherlessness increases the odds of criminal behavior and then goes on to acknowledge that...
(2) There is a high correlation between fatherlessness and violence.

But it's "clear," we're told, that there needs to be "more research" before a link between fatherlessness and mass shooters can be established? Exactly what additional "research" added to the already powerful evidence connecting fatherlessness to violence do such writers need?

While we wait for more studies to satisfy every commentator, every "expert" — studies which may never take place — it's likely that large numbers of people will continue to die because... why?? Because this commentator isn't yet sure that fatherlessness is actually linked to the violence he already says its linked to??

This is the same logic that we constantly see among those denying the pervasive, lifelong damage of fatherlessness. Let's just say we need "more studies!"[1]

Note that "experts" are consistently cautious that they don't make definitive pronouncements, except to say that others disagreeing with them are wrong in their thinking. While admitting to the likely results of fatherlessness in one thing or another, they nonetheless continue to call for more studies and more research.

Well, we've had enough.

What many don't know is that some of the questions we would like answered *cannot* be answered in many *ethical* research designs. There are limits. Simply accepting personal reports from parents and children is problematic. In-home observations are little better.

Defining what makes good fathering or a good family is nearly impossible in itself since it can vary among families. We can only do what we can do. Too many times, both here and elsewhere, some research designs themselves can and should be called into question. All this can lead to inaccurate or, minimally, misleading research results. We may not even be asking the right questions in the first place.

At this point, we may have close to about all we can easily get without causing what are now effectively unconscionable delays or employing questionable research designs. Based on countless observations, past data, and sensibilities, it's time to stop defaulting to the "more research" mantra. We should assume that it is truly a problem, and finally address it head-on.

These research concerns are not limited to fatherlessness. They spread across other areas including education, a special concern of this author. See the book, *Education Is Dead,* also by this author.

We don't have time to wait as we indulge what has effectively now become foolishness. Sure, I like studies. They're fascinating and often help to set the road ahead. So, go ahead! Have more studies!

But here's the thing:

Don't wait a single day longer attempting to address unhealthy fathers and unhealthy families. *Not a single day longer.* Ignore those people who don't seem to have had real world connections with the sadness and damage of fatherlessness. Many of the rest of us either have had personal experience with it, or have seen it in others.

Ignore the absurd definitions put forward so that children can be defined as having fathers when they clearly don't have one in the meaning we and others put forth — as *fathering*, not simply the physical presence of a father. Actual fathering, *good* fathering, is needed to ensure that children are raised to be healthy, responsible, and hopefully (but no guarantees here), happy adults.

Countless children are still effectively fatherless even though they technically have a father living at home. *Presence* does not equal fathering. Only good and consistent *fathering* by a good, *hopefully biological* father (as some data tells us) will meet the true definition of being well-raised by a good father.

Being a good father isn't easy. I'm not at all suggesting that it's anything but hard, sometimes very hard. But it's only that which will lead to great children becoming great adults.

Remember, too, that even in the case of a good and loving father, if there is a serious problem with the mother or with their parents' relationship, all of which can equate to a dysfunctional family, bad things can still result.

Some argue that since people have not been able to fix the decline in marriage and continued rise of single parent families, it's a waste of time to even try addressing marriage or single parent issues. Therefore, many people seem to suggest, let's move on to handle the "real" problem: guns.

They seem to say, "There is nothing we ("you") can do about fatherlessness and other family problems, so let's move on and talk about my personal agenda items." This may be the most common way to ignore and move on from the many statistically valid reports of the damage of fatherlessness.

The definition of fatherlessness in the book you're now reading uses a tough definition. It has to. It's the only definition that fits actual killers.

The bottom line here is that, with just a few possible exceptions, killers are indeed fatherless. Those who waste time doubting it, arguing against it, or are in outright denial, ensure future delays that will see yet more people die. Stop the dying. Start fixing this now.

Another site reviewing claims of fatherlessness says that it reviewed news reports to find if "any" shooters grew up in a household with a father and found that a number did. Using a loose definition of fatherhood, it then apparently determined that those killers were not fatherless at all, as some had claimed.

What does it mean to be a "father?" A biological contribution and an irritable presence watching TV all day with a beer in hand and being bothered every time one of his children approaches too closely? For purposes of determining whether a child grew up with a father, that would hardly qualify. That is not fathering.

Yet that is what too many commentators and reporters assume constitutes a child being "raised" by a real father.

A pervasive problem is that people concerned about fatherlessness can't easily talk to others who may not be concerned. The definitions of fatherlessness are so different that people aren't talking about the same thing.

Remember that too many children actually suffer from a lack of fathering, "fatheringlessness," not necessarily a lack of a father. Barring issues of abuse or the presence of other serious concerns, fathering is almost always best coming from a child's actual biological father, not a "father figure," though sometimes that's all we've got for our children.

---

1. I'll note here that referencing that particular article or author isn't needed for the purposes here. To do so invites consideration of that single article. In fact, I use what it says as emblematic of the same thinking among many other articles and authors.

This and several following sections are taken, adapted, or abridged from the 2022 edition of the author's book:
THE CARTAINOS
MEN OF PASSION • MEN OF STONE.

CHAPTER FOUR
Insights Into Absent Fathers

Although the coming sections are taken from the epic saga, *The Cartainos: Men of Passion • Men of Stone,* do not misunderstand the family talked about in that book. The violence about which the book in your hands talks was not present among the Cartaino family in the book about them, but the issue of fatherlessness clearly affected that family.

Note that the definition of fatherlessness in the quoted research of these adapted sections may be different from that as used elsewhere in this book.

Even though our book here is about killers who are generally sons, to fully understand the power and need for fathers, we must be aware of their impact on all of their children — including their daughters.

One more caveat. Regardless of what is said in this book, I recognize that there are some fathers who are emotionally cold. They may seem to have no love within them. Some are even dangerous. But those are a small minority of fathers. Most are quite the opposite.

Note that since these sections were originally written, the situation in certain areas regarding fathers has worsened. However, I have kept the details and statistics from the original writing. Let's begin.

***

There is one thing that seems to have had a particularly negative impact on the inner level of satisfaction, on the frustrations, and the loss of love in many individuals [in the Cartaino family]. Simultaneously, it impacted the preservation of generational knowledge and the connection to ancestors and family history. It is not reaching too far to suggest that it might be the single most critical thing that led to so much sadness throughout the history of this family, especially among the family's daughters.

That one thing is the loss or absence of fathers.

The pain and difficulties these fathers' children have suffered, and continue to suffer — especially their daughters — cannot be overstated. Emotional and other damage caused by fatherlessness lasts a lifetime.

Yet children often don't understand the origins of these things in their lives. Even as adults, many can be internally foggy, while still feeling fully functional. They may think that all is well with them, even when something isn't. They don't know that anything is wrong or missing, because they grew up without the things a good father could have given to them.

The absence of involved, caring fathers living with their families is one of the most serious issues in America and the world today. It is destroying lives and societies everywhere. It is best thought of as a pandemic — because it is.

***

The information in this section relates especially to families in America today. Here we will, in part:

(1) Look at some statistics on the damage caused by the crisis of fatherlessness;

(2) Take a brief look at fatherhood and some causes of fatherlessness;

(3) Consider some fatherless sons in history; and

(4) Note the critical connection between fatherhood and marriage.

Later in the book will be thoughts on how to address this crisis.

Before beginning and in spite of what follows, let me state that there are indeed times when children should not be raised by one or both of their biological parents.

Sadly, we know that being raised by a bad parent can and does happen to too many children. Based on reports from her oldest daughters, [one of the mothers in The Cartainos] appeared to have done irreparable damage to her husband, her marriage, and her children. Those reports appear to show that that one mother's decisions, parenting, and seeming lack of love would ensure sadness and difficult lives for her children throughout their lives.

CHAPTER FIVE
The Damage of Fatherlessness

The headline in a 2013 article said: *"Lack of Father Figure Triggers Risky Sexual Behavior Among Young Girls."*[1] That is unfortunate wording because, while often better than no father at all, families don't need "father figures." They need actual fathers. Whenever possible, that means *biological* fathers.

The book, *Fatherless America* (1996), by David Blankenhorn, is subtitled, "Confronting Our Most Urgent Social Problem." The more one researches this, the more one understands the truth of that observation.

The Fatherless Daughter Project: Understanding Our Losses and Reclaiming Our Lives (2016), by Denna Babul, RN, and Karin Luise, contains descriptions of the many difficulties with which fatherless daughters struggle in their lives.

It also observes that, as adults, many fatherless daughters are strong women (at least externally). That is supported by both the words and observations of some fatherless daughters in the Cartaino family. Whether that's good or bad depends on one's point of view.

However, co-author, Denna Babul, is clear about her bottom line: *"The loss of my father was the defining moment in my life."*

We soon realize that what we currently hear from some of the "educated experts" in our constantly changing social and cultural world may not be giving us a full or correct understanding of all of this.

The National Fatherhood Initiative [NFI] is a respected source for data on absent fathers.[2] Founded in 1994, the non-profit National Fatherhood Initiative is a significant resource for fatherhood research, statistics, and training. It encourages sharing statistics on the national and worldwide crisis of absent fathers:

> *In the U.S., children raised without a father in the home are more likely to have behavioral problems, commit crime, and go to prison. They are more likely to face abuse and neglect and more likely to abuse drugs and alcohol. They have twice the risk of infant mortality.*

Such children are also:

> Twice as likely to suffer from obesity;
> Twice as likely to drop out of high school;
> At four times greater risk of poverty; and
> Seven times more likely to become pregnant as a
>   teen.

Quoting from the U.S. Census Bureau (2018), *Father Facts, Eighth Edition*, reports that, in 2018, 26.5% of children in the U.S. lived in a "father-absent" home (down slightly from 27.2% in 2016).[3] But compare those numbers with the 11.2% figure in 1960. These numbers vary substantially when we look at various ethnic groups:[4]

Among Black children, 48.1% lived only with their mother;
Among Hispanic children, 24.9%;
Among White children, 17.4% lived only with their mother;
Among Asians, just 8.5%.

Statistics on the actual damage of fatherlessness can vary a lot depending on the source and the year. Regardless, they all point to a critical problem. They all point to a devastating scarring of children and society. In fact, the damage due to absent fathers is even worse than the numbers tell us.

Beyond the numbers we just saw, the non-profit National Center for Fathering[5] adds, *"Millions more [children] have dads who are physically present, but emotionally absent."*[6]

Established in 1990, the National Center for Fathering [NCF] is a significant source for resources and training in support of fathers. The NCF notes that if fatherlessness were a disease, it would be a national emergency.

Some older statistics on the NCF site include:[7]

70% of teen pregnancies happen in fatherless homes;

80% of adolescents in psychiatric hospitals come from fatherless homes;

90% of all homeless and runaway children are from fatherless homes;

Those from fatherless homes are twice as likely to commit suicide;

Children are nine times more likely to be raped or abused in a home without a biological father.

Other negative behaviors are also associated with absent biological fathers. For example, *Father Facts, Eighth Edition*, reports:

• *The absence of a biological father is a significant predictor for exposure to child abuse and neglect for children.*

• *Father absence is a predictor for children engaging in criminal activity.*

• *The absence of a father is associated with lower levels of children's educational attainment.*

• *Father absence, as well as the quality of the father-child relationship, impacts children as young as toddler age and continues to lead to adverse behavioral outcomes through adolescence.*

. . .

My belief and observations are that such impacts extend well beyond adolescence. They can affect children throughout the entirety of their lives.

Other aspects of children's lives that may be affected include the quality of children's physical health, higher poverty levels, and a "significant impact" on sexual activity and teen pregnancy.

Father Facts, Eighth Edition (2019; or available later editions) is highly recommended for extensive data on fatherlessness and related issues.

***

A *Wall Street Journal* article[8] of June 2, 2017, referenced a study by Danielle DelPriore, Gabriel Schlomer, and Bruce Ellis, published in *Developmental Psychology*.[9] The study looked at the impact of absent or low-quality fathering on how parental monitoring affects risky sexual behaviors of daughters.

The study also referenced an example of another behavior that can affect daughters.

After some fathers left, and after the divorce, it observed that some "mother-daughter relationships may experience qualitative changes" that might contribute to daughters' risky behaviors. It continued:

> For instance, mothers frequently discuss sensitive topics with their daughters following a divorce, including sharing financial concerns and expressing negative views toward their former spouse. Such disclosures may have negative implications for the closeness of mother-daughter relationships as well as for daughters' well-being.[10] Specifically, the frequency and depth of maternal disclosures have been shown to predict increases in daughters' psychological distress, negativity toward marriage, behavioral problems (e.g., substance use), and dating behaviors.[11]

. . .

This suggests yet another parental action that can negatively affect a daughter. Is this action the mother's doing? Of course, it is.

However, in looking at it, one cannot deny that this links to the father's absence, even if the blame for his absence does not entirely rest on him.

So, in some cases, a daughter might be emotionally imperiled not only because a father is absent or provides low-quality fathering, but also because of a mother's response to that absence.

***

Fatherlessness, low-quality fathering, or a mother's inappropriate response to a father can all negatively affect the lives of children.

The earlier referenced study by DelPriore, Schlomer, and Ellis (May 2017), stated that *"a robust association has been observed between fathering quality and sexual risk-taking among adolescent girls."* Other studies agree.

Although not addressed in the study, those working with adolescent girls are aware that such behaviors, often accompanied by issues of low self-image, frequently follow them into adulthood.

Additionally, *The Wall Street Journal* article lends support that there are times when *"a divorce may be less harmful for a girl than more years with a bad dad."*

Separate from that May 2017 study, we note here that damage to girls is not limited to sexual risk-taking. In adulthood, it can carry over to other areas. Some fatherless daughters, as adults, might find themselves choosing non-traditional lifestyles.

For example, some may consciously choose a non-traditional lifestyle living on the streets, among similar examples. Such lifestyles may also involve regular abuse of drugs or alcohol, as well as short-term, non-committed relationships.

In the end, such choices are likely to prove harmful both to themselves and to others, including to their own children. Rarely do fatherless daughters recognize ongoing harm soon enough, if at all, while involved in potentially unhealthy lifestyles. Without that recognition, positive and healthy changes are rarely made.

Multiple other studies confirm increased levels of promiscuity among women raised without a father's involvement. In addition, they often have unfulfilling romantic relationships with men.

It may not be a coincidence that one Cartaino father's three oldest children, who all lost their father while very young, had a total of at least thirteen marriages among them. Seven were reported for his oldest daughter, alone.

Each of his next two children had three marriages each. Those add to at least one long-term relationship that others had assumed was a marriage. Those numbers far exceed the combined marriages of most other [Cartaino] children, where we mostly saw greater paternal involvement.

Beyond just the number of marriages are the numbers of unfortunate choices as that one father's descendants, especially the women, selected spouses. Without the example and accepted counsel of involved fathers, his children, grandchildren, great-grandchildren, and even beyond, suffered difficulties in marriages in what may be larger than expected numbers. That pattern is borne out in multiple studies of fatherless children.

Shortcomings on both sides often complicate such marital failures. Things in life are not one-sided, and the full truth about any relationship is rarely known.

Wherever one might choose to assign blame within each relationship, the one thing they often had in common, through multiple generations, was the lack of strong, involved, and loving fathers present in the lives of their daughters.

Some developmental damage may not occur when divorced/single mothers demonstrate strong and caring parenting, to include active parental monitoring of their children. Yet, even then, fatherless children are not likely to escape damage as they grow into adulthood.

As we repeatedly add, damaged children are found even in intact, two-parent families, and stable, apparently well-adjusted children may be found in many single-parent families.

Nonetheless, enormously higher risks for children exist when a father is missing. Most children — especially daughters — in the lines of the [Cartaino] family appear to have been significantly affected.

In the end, we might find that none escape.

✱✱✱

Irresponsibly, some choose to minimize the problem. Working with a different agenda, these people prefer to shift the focus away from fatherlessness. They either don't know, or prefer to ignore, the compelling body of evidence surrounding this issue.

Of course, life is not simple. Other issues contribute to this and to every problem. But some of these naysayers seem to suggest that fatherlessness is not as critical as it is. They give simplistic solutions that have been repeatedly shown not to work. They prefer to bring up other issues that seem to be part of some personal agenda. Such people only contribute to the problem. [12]

---

1. As published in the Daily Mail (UK): *dailymail.co.uk/femail/article-2340431/Do-absent-dads-make-promiscuous-daughters-Study-finds-lack-father-figure-triggers-risky-sexual-behavior-young-girls.html*. Accessed Oct. 22, 2019.

2. See the website: *fatherhood.org*. Accessed December 23, 2017.

3. As per: *Father Facts, Eighth Edition (National Fatherhood Initiative; 2019), Appendix A.*

4. Quoting other statistics from the Census Bureau (each year and analysis give different numbers), the Fatherhood Factor stated that "23.6% of US children (17.4 million) lived in father-absent homes in 2014." Regardless of which year and which statistics are quoted, the numbers are enormous and frightening.

   The above is at the website: *fatherhoodfactor.com/us-fatherless-statistics*, accessed May 17, 2019. It references the US Census Bureau, 2015, "*Living arrangements of children under 18 years and marital status of parents, by age, sex, race, and Hispanic origin and selected characteristics of the child for all children: 2014."* Accessed December 23, 2017.

5.   See the website: *fathers.com.* Accessed December 23, 2017.

6.   Found   at: *fathers.com/statistics-and-research/the-extent-of-fatherlessness.* Accessed August 18, 2017.

7.   See: *fathers.com/wp39/wp-content/uploads/2015/05/fatherlessInfographic.png. Accessed Aug 18, 2017.* The website contained references for the statistics. Although some studies are now older, the connections and concerns linked to absent fathers remain the same. Some children in those earlier, quoted studies are now adults and, we surmise, might still be experiencing the effects of a missing father in their lives.

8.   The Link Between Detached Dads and Risk-Taking Girls (*New research on daughters and risk-taking sexual behavior) by Melvin Konner, The Wall Street Journal, June 2, 2017.*

9.   *DelPriore, D. J., Schlomer, G. L., & Ellis, B. J. (2017, May 8). Impact of Fathers on Parental Monitoring of Daughters and Their Affiliation With Sexually Promiscuous Peers: A Genetically and Environmentally Controlled Sibling Study. Developmental Psychology. Advance online publication.* Website: *dx.doi.org/10.1037/dev0000327.* Site accessed November 5, 2019.

10.   The study referenced here was found in the study: *"Koerner, S. S., Wallace, S., Lehman, S. J., & Raymond, M. (2002). Mother-to-daughter disclosure after divorce: Are there costs and benefits? Journal of Child and Family Studies, 11, 469–483. Website: dx.doi.org/10.1023/A:1020987509405."* Accessed Aug 5, 2017.

11.   Studies referenced here were found in the following: *"Dennison, R. P., & Koerner, S. S. (2006). Post-divorce interparental conflict and adolescents' attitudes about marriage: The influence of maternal disclosures and adolescent gender. Journal of Divorce & Re-marriage, 45 (1–2), 31–49. dx.doi.org/10.1300/J087v45n01_02; Koerner, S. S., Kenyon, D. B., & Rankin, L. A. (2006). Growing up faster? Post-divorce catalysts in the mother-adolescent relationship. Journal of Divorce & Remarriage, 45, 25– 41. dx.doi.org/10.1300/ J087v45n03_02; Koerner, S. S., Wallace, S., Lehman, S. J., Lee, S. A., & Escalante, K. A. (2004). Sensitive mother-to-adolescent disclosures after divorce: Is the experience of sons different from that of daughters? Journal of Family Psychology, 18, 46–57. Website: doi.apa.org/doiLanding? doi=10.1037/0893-3200.18.1.46."* Accessed Aug 5, 2017.

12.   As one example, see (or don't see) an article appearing in The Washington Post on January 10, 2017: "The Dangerous Myth Of The 'Missing Black Father'." Preferring to blame racism, the article's subtitle tells us, *"Responsible fatherhood only goes so far in a world plagued by institutionalized oppression."* We also hear about *"the* supposed *absence of black fathers."* (*Emphasis added.*) Supposed? At times, that author appears to present fatherlessness as though it only exists within the black community. Although the problem is especially severe there, it affects all peoples everywhere.

This section is taken from:
THE CARTAINOS.

CHAPTER SIX
Fathers and Causes of Fatherlessness

For our purposes here, children are "fatherless" if a good (generally biological) father had not been actively with them as they grew into a full or mature adult. Sometimes, a stepfather or someone else might step in to finish the process successfully, but the odds of such success are much lower, especially when a child is older.

That doesn't mean that all children who become full or mature adults with their fathers present are necessarily good and wonderful people. It just means a "full or mature adult," however that might be defined. Such definitions do not include any of the differing and evolving definitions of what a "legal" adult is. An actual adult is different and generally older than a societally defined, legal adult.

For example, for purposes of voting, signing contracts, and other things, a "legal" adult has been redefined from a 21-year-old to an 18-year-old in the United States. But those still-young, redefined adults are rarely "full or mature" adults. They are still growing and maturing.[1]

Other sources mentioned here, including statistics quoted earlier, may presume a different definition as to what a "full or mature adult" might be.

✲✲

Most people can list many reasons why a father might be absent. However, the reasons are often less important than the damage done when children grow up without their father.

How are fathers lost? A father might die before his children finish growing up, perhaps even before his children are born. Fathers are lost to illness and accidents. Too many are incarcerated. Of course, most think that the most significant loss of fathers would be through divorce.

However, there is something else that is becoming even more common.

**

Especially in [the Cartaino family in the first half of the 1900s], there was a stigma in the social culture of America — a feeling of shame — when a child was born out-of-wedlock. That same stigma still exists in many countries and cultures today, even in America.

Of course, the child had parents, but the child's parents weren't married. Sometimes the father wasn't present at all.

Not only was an out-of-wedlock birth an embarrassment for the woman, but sometimes also for the man. Some women hid the fact that they were not married...even from their child. Children born out-of-wedlock are still sometimes referred to as being "illegitimate."

An October 17, 2018, article in *The New York Post*,[2] referred to a 2018 United Nations report.[3] It said that 40% of babies born in the United States were born to unmarried mothers in 2015. That contrasts with just over 10% born out-of-wedlock in 1970. Numbers in other countries were even worse. The 2015 figure in France was 60%.

It is clear from this that vast numbers of children are born without committed fathers from the moment of their birth.

Another study found that, in America today, the majority of children born to women under 30 years old are born out-of-wedlock. At least one major publication referred to this as "the new normal."[4] The future is likely to see the same for others, too.

This may now be common, but does it go too far to call it "normal?" Studies continue to show that children born out-of-wedlock have a much more difficult life ahead of them than do those born to married parents who raise them together. So do their mothers.

The numbers of this increasing trend over the past decades, do point to something approaching a dangerous new normal — and these numbers have been growing. More recently, out-of-wedlock births among Black Americans have been reported to be at 70%.

Clearly, out-of-wedlock births have already long since passed divorce as the leading cause of fatherlessness in some segments of American society, as well as in some other countries.

Lending further support to a reduced moral stigma in America, a May 2017 Gallup poll[5] found that 62% of those surveyed felt that having a baby outside of marriage was "morally acceptable." The percentage of those finding such births to be morally acceptable has been rising in America for many years.

A Gallup poll of May 2002 found that 45% (*compared to 62% in 2017*) felt that having a baby outside of marriage was acceptable. Yet even that 45% is high when compared to society's morality of not many generations before.

***

Books on fatherlessness appear to dwell more on the issue of daughters than on sons, although both are clearly affected by growing up without quality, involved fathers in their lives.

Where fathers remain in the family, connecting positively with their children, generational damage is often reduced. But, in some cases, the loss of even a single father seems to cause significant damage not just to that one father's children — but to his children's children and continuing on to still more generations.

Many times, children blame their father for leaving them, for not being there for them. Seemingly fewer times, they blame their mother. Of course, to children, it's all about them. The world revolves around them. That's understandable. They are just children.

Most people today are at least partly aware of this widespread and damaging problem. The question remains, what can be done to turn it around? On a broader societal basis, the disappointing answer generally seems to be — nothing.

Sure, efforts are being made to address the problem of father-lessness. And those efforts should continue. But they have not been enough. With exceptions, most "efforts" are lip service — nothing more than a passing acknowledgment of the problem before moving on to other things.

We will look at some options later in the book.

The presence of stepparents, or individual efforts by the remaining parent, have not been enough to compensate for the loss of fathers.

This is not meant to devalue good stepparents or the good work of single parents. Regardless of any difficulties, all must do their best so that those whose lives they influence will have a better chance for a good life ahead. Sadly, statistics show that their success in doing that is rarely enough. Of course, as much as some try, no parent is perfect.

Too many children endure difficult lives as they grow up and move into adulthood. We cannot know for sure what would have been different had a secure and loving father been actively present in the lives of fatherless children. But their lives would likely have been more positive, including in their understanding of others and also in a healthier ability to give and receive love.

Seldom are most of us aware when the paths of our lives were determined, when we were put on one path rather than another. Most children don't know either.

✳✳✳

Vast numbers of people today continue to place the primary responsibility — and blame — directly on fathers for not being around as their children grow up. While accurate at times, it is wrong and unfair to fathers far more often than people realize.

Even though our focus is on fathers here, far too many mothers are unfit or unable to raise children than most of us would like to think.

Some adult children and grandchildren in the broader family of [the Cartainos] looked back and placed a significant part of the blame for the absence of their fathers directly on their mother or grandmother.

We can't expect either parent to be perfect. We are all imperfect people doing the best we can in life. We should all be more patient and forgiving of each other than we see most people are today.

Except for fathers who might create a dangerous or unusually bad environment for their children, almost all children would be better served having their fathers regularly present throughout their lives. Of course, truly bad fathers can do terrible long-term damage to children — as much as damage may be caused by truly bad mothers, many would argue.

I do not take the position that a father who consistently acts against the best interests of his children should have the responsibility for them — especially if a good mother is around. But the presence and positive involvement of a non-abusive[6] father is so important that all reasonable efforts should be made to maintain that father's consistent and positive presence and involvement in his children's lives.

Fathers who relinquish their responsibilities through a debilitating use of drugs or alcohol, or by physical abuse that endangers both children and spouse are a separate issue. But the vast majority of fathers are not like that.

Here, too, we do not look at the reverse of this: the damage done by bad, even dangerous children and grandchildren to their parents and grandparents. But we acknowledge the existence of this serious issue.

All fathers are not good fathers. But some legitimately good fathers are sometimes judged as "bad" because of some well-meaning — perhaps even correct — parental action they may have taken that was wrongly or unfairly judged as bad by a child or a child's mother. Even a handful of such wrongly-judged words or actions can condemn what may actually be a good father forever. We are also not considering that complexity here.

Sadly, there appears to be an unsettling increase in the numbers of incompetent, even dangerous parents — both mothers and fathers. This is often due to parents no longer knowing how to be a parent because they themselves were raised with unhealthy or missing parents.

Today, increasingly large numbers of people who become parents have been raised with no moral foundation, often without God, and with no sense that it is important to be a good person and to care about others.

Missing fathers and bad parenting from either parent who do not have an instilled moral code for goodness, as well as a faith in God, as traditionally understood, is self-perpetuating. It destroys them, their children, those who step into their lives, and society in general. Too often, their children then continue in that pattern in their own lives.

****

Can a relationship with a father when a child is much older (an older teenager and beyond) make up for not having one earlier? Rarely. Sure, they can and should develop a friendship — hopefully much more. A relationship with a good father is important at any age. A child can still learn things about family history and many other things from a father later in life. But the die has generally been cast well before then.

As a father spends time with a now-adult child, he often finds that his real value in helping to raise his child has been largely lost. Of course, his child may not see or understand that. Children — especially younger ones, but also those older — are generally only concerned about themselves.

However, children themselves — whether still growing or fully grown — should do all that they can to regularly spend positive and connected time with their fathers (and their mothers, too, should that need to be said).

***

We have mentioned the damage to daughters here because so many of them appear to be damaged. But we also know that sons are seriously affected, especially in terms of the most serious violence. We will see that clearly in the next chapter.

Multiple books and studies point to lasting damage to sons that frequently includes issues of increased violence. In his book, *Fatherless Generation, Redeeming the Story,* John Sowers says:[7]

> *The rampant spread of gangs in our country is the direct result of fatherlessness. Demographically speaking, the most reliable predictor for gang activity and youth violence is...fatherlessness.*

Having worked with gang members, I add that some of their fathers also grew up in violent environments. In many cases, their fathers grew up without fathers themselves. Such children's fathers may be around their children, but they do not necessarily reign in the undesirable activities of their sons. They may not know how to be the father their children need.

So, even in instances where fatherlessness skips a generation, earlier damage often passes forward.

Apart from issues involving higher levels of violence, fatherlessness can also negatively affect the performance of sons (and daughters) in their education and in other parts of their lives.

---

1. Of course, some people never become "full or mature adults," no matter what their age.

2. New York Post: *More babies are being born to unmarried parents in the U.S. than ever, according to Laura Italiano, October 17, 2018.*

3. *The State Of World Population 2018, Figure 35: Percentage of births outside marriage in the European Union and selected countries, 1970–2016.* The UN reports said that many children born out-of-wedlock were born to unmarried couples living together. The report documented situations worldwide, not solely in the United States.

4. Found in: For Women Under 30, Most Births Occur Outside Marriage, *By Jason Deparle and Sabrina Tavernise, The New York Times, February 17, 2012.* For a related perspective, see: For Millennials, Out-of-Wedlock Childbirth Is the Norm, *Slate, June 23, 2014.*

5. *Americans' Opinions About Moral Acceptability of Practices, May 2017, Gallup.*

6. The definition and full discussion of an "abusive" or "non-abusive" parent is beyond the scope of this writing. But "abuse" should not necessarily be assumed to include the many all-encompassing, politically-correct definitions increasingly suggested by many well-intentioned, but wrongly-focused people who have sought to prohibit almost any kind of needed guidance and correction by parents, educators, and even the military. Such people often include politicians and judges. The definitions of "abuse" and other sociological terms have been "flexible and evolving" over the years and across generations. How one person understands such terms often differs from how another person understands those same terms.

7. *Sowers, John A.* "Fatherless Generation: Redeeming the Story." (*Zondervan*; 2010).

This important section is also from:
THE CARTAINOS.
The serious violence about which the book in your hands talks was not present in the Cartaino family.

CHAPTER SEVEN
Fatherless Sons

S o, just how important *are* good fathers? If you have had doubts about this issue, the fatherless sons in this chapter can make you a believer.

Many boys brought up without a father can turn out fine anyway. There are many of them. The internationally lauded Dr. Ben Carson, M.D., is at the high end of many such examples. Dr. Carson credits much of his success to his mother, Sonya Carson (1928-2017). Her persistence, strength, caring, and example, as well as her insistence on the importance of reading — she herself could not read — set him on a road for success in medicine and beyond.[1]

Others have similar stories.

But we also know that too many sons who are brought up without a father before their sons finish maturing — or with a bad father — sometimes exhibit serious behavioral problems, even as adults. Not all sons have mothers who can step up as successfully as Sonya Carson did.

Even in homes with men who appear to be good fathers, an overall seriously dysfunctional family environment can still lead to bad outcomes. In some cases, their sons can show, among other things, a higher level of anger or violence than do sons raised in healthier family environments. Today, some join gangs. In this section, we'll look at some sons who did not have healthy fathers and families.

Even after reaching adulthood, some can become a danger to themselves, to others, and to society. As has been said before, issues of fatherlessness can last well into adulthood, even a lifetime. The self-control and moral foundations these sons need may never develop.[2] But, sometimes, things get much worse.

Even sons with both parents present often have parents not adequately involved in their upbringing. Parents may both work and be too busy or too tired to give strong, loving, and properly-involved parenting. Especially when their child is older, they may not oversee what their child is doing, who their child is around, where their child goes online and, generally, provide little or no oversight and appropriate rearing.

Therefore, it can be true that children can grow up fatherless even when a father is technically present in the house.

As has already been said, fathers really don't understand their critical importance in providing definitive love, oversight, teaching, and example. A father who is raising children as a single parent has additional issues. (Mothers, I'm not ignoring you. I'm talking about fathers here.)

A reminder that, for our purposes here, children are "fatherless" if a good — generally biological — father had not been with his children during effectively all the years when they were growing to adulthood. Actual ages at what might appropriately be considered adulthood vary. It's generally not 18.

Below are just a few examples of men and boys who grew up with bad or absent biological fathers. Can what we find here be blamed on fatherlessness alone? Likely not alone, but it's almost assuredly a foundational factor. In light of this, it would be foolish not to understand the importance of good fathers being consistently in the lives of their children.

There are countless other examples of sons raised without their biological fathers — of wrong paths taken by those with absent, bad, or low-quality fathers. Here, I mention a few of the worst. But we must ask ourselves how many truly bad people are not mentioned here? And might those names left out be fatherless, too?

Specific information on each of those listed here has been

gleaned from various sources. As more unfolds, some information might change. Nonetheless, it's believed that the commonality linking those mentioned below will be evident regardless.

****

Let's start with:

Joseph Stalin (1878-1953): Although Joseph Stalin's father may have begun as a good and respected man, he sank into alcoholism. He began beating his young son, often for no reason. His father left Stalin's mother and moved to a different town. When Stalin was around 11 years old, he had his last significant contact with his father.[3]

Stalin was the second leader of the Soviet Union, after Vladimir Lenin. Estimates of those killed or allowed to die during Stalin's brutal regime conflict. Some range from around 10 to 20 million people. Other estimates go well beyond that. Stanford history Professor Norman Naimark clearly identifies the killings and mass murders under Stalin's regime as genocides.[4]

Note that deaths caused by both Stalin and the other sons listed below do not include other crimes and atrocities which many also committed.

Norman Naimark says that Stalin's "difficult family background" as he grew up, was one of several moments that would later lead to the suffering and death of countless people.

Could anything have stopped his brutality? Would a different upbringing have put him on a better path? We can't know. Life is complicated. But sometimes changing a single foundational cog can change everything.

Had he remained with his father, it's possible that "Soso" (one of Stalin's names as a youth) would have become a shoemaker, like his father or perhaps something else.[5] One can certainly surmise that millions of deaths might have been prevented.

This is another example of the pattern of absent and damaged fathers. Within that pattern, we see the terrible path taken by this fatherless son.

Here are more fatherless sons in the order of their birth:

ATTILA THE HUN (Born circa 406 A.D. Some give earlier years. Died in 453): Attila's early life is uncertain. However, according to WorldHistory.org, Mundzuk, Attila's father, appears to *"...have died early"* in the lives of Attila and his older brother, Bleda.[6] (Years later, Attila is believed to have killed his brother.) Their uncle, Rua, would become king. The brothers both lived beside their uncle until his death. Eventually, Attila ruled. As with other things from those early times, the number of deaths for which Attila was responsible is unknown. A quote attributed to Attila says: *"There, where I have passed, the grass will never grow again."*[7]

Ghengis Khan (circa 1162-1227): Ghengis Khan's father was poisoned and died when his son was nine years old. Ghengis Khan was the first leader of the powerful Mongol Empire. He's considered the founder of Mongolia. Estimates of the number of deaths for which he is responsible vary from 20 to 40 million people.

Ivan the Terrible (1530-1584): Ivan the Terrible's father, Grand Duke Vasily, died when Ivan was three years old. His mother died when he was eight, likely poisoned. When he was 17, he married Anastasia, his first wife. But, after 13 years of marriage, she was also poisoned (though presumably not by Ivan) and died.

Known as Tsar Ivan IV, Ivan the Terrible was the first tsar of Russia. What are likely conservative estimates of deaths under Ivan the Terrible range from 60,000 to well over 200,000 people. Beyond the numbers, the terror and brutality by which many of them were killed are particularly remembered.

It's certainly likely that, had he been raised by his father rather than by the often sadistic boyars (part of Russia's old aristocracy), things may well have been different. The boyars set him on a bad path.

I must add that there are different substantively competing historical narratives about Ivan The Terrible. I am not weighing in on those narratives here. Historians do acknowledge that he defended Russia from some of its enemies, but it's generally not in that light for which he is remembered today. In our context, it's enough to know that Ivan IV did do some terrible things — and that he had grown up fatherless.

Although unconfirmed, towards the end of his life it has long been rumored that, in a fit of anger, he killed his own son whom he had loved and who would have succeeded him.

Vladimir Lenin (1870-1924): Vladimir Lenin's father died when his son was 15 years old. Notably, after his father's death, Lenin's behavior changed significantly — for the worse. Lenin became the first leader of the Soviet Union (1917-1924). Estimates of deaths for which Lenin was responsible vary widely, going upwards to well beyond three million people. (Some estimates place the number lower.)

Here are more examples:

Adolf Hitler (1889-1945): Adolf Hitler's father died when he was 13 years old. Ruler of Germany and the Nazi Party, Hitler was responsible for the deaths of tens of millions of people. Beyond the millions killed in the Holocaust, many lay the entire Second World War in Europe and Russia at his feet.

Mao Zedong [Mao Tse-tung] (1893-1976): Mao was at odds with his father when young and reportedly finally left home at age 16. The story and legitimacy of most things dealing with Mao Zedong depend on who is doing the talking. The infamous leader of China's Great Leap Forward and Cultural Revolution is still defended by many Chinese people, seemingly both in and out of China. Nonetheless, numerous sources suggest that the number of deaths, due to both the policies under his rule and his personal animus, ranges widely from 40 to 80 million people.[8] Mao's supporters frequently deny both those numbers and that the responsibility for them belongs primarily to Mao Zedong.

Pol Pot (1925-1998): Pol Pot was six years old when he was sent to live with wealthier relatives. That wasn't necessarily unusual in Cambodia at the time. Nonetheless, his birth father didn't raise him. He became the communist leader of Cambodia and of the Khmer Rouge (from 1963 to 1997). He was responsible for the deaths of over one and a half million people.

Idi Amin (1925-2003): Idi Amin's father left him and his mother around the time of Idi Amin's birth. His mother's family raised him. Idi Amin was the President of Uganda from 1971 to 1979. Estimates of deaths for which he was responsible range from 300,000 to 500,000 people. He was known as the Butcher of Uganda.

.   .   .

Fidel Castro (1926-2016): Fidel Castro was born out-of-wedlock. He was sent away from home to live with a teacher when he was just six years old. His father stayed at home. Although Fidel periodically returned home for holidays and other visits, he remained with that teacher for years while he went to school. Later, he also lived at boarding schools. However, even had he been home more often, his father, Angel (1875-1956), was not reported to be a good father.[9] An accurate estimate of the number of deaths for which Fidel Castro was later responsible isn't easily known. Along with other things about Fidel Castro, data depend on which side of the Cuban political spectrum the one offering the data is on.

Saddam Hussein (1937-2006): Saddam Hussein's father died while his mother was still pregnant with him. He lived with his uncle and, of course, never knew his father. Saddam Hussein was the president of Iraq from 1979 until 2003. He was found guilty of crimes against humanity and executed in 2006. The number of deaths for which he is responsible is not fully known. Depending on source, they likely number at least half a million but, when taking torture, starvation, and other methods of death into account, may have easily exceeded a million victims.

Osama Bin Laden (1957-2011): Osama Bin Laden's birth father divorced Bin Laden's mother not long after he was born. Depending on the source, his father died when Bin Laden was 12 or 13 years old. His mother remarried. The boy was brought up by his stepfather.

Osama Bin Laden was the leader of the terrorist group, Al Qaeda. Until his death at the hands of American military forces, he was responsible for the deaths of thousands of people.

• • •

There are also these:

Charles Manson (1934-2017): Manson's mother had filed a paternity suit against his father. Charles Manson may have never known his biological father. He became the head of the infamous cult known as the "Manson Family." Members of the Manson Family were convicted of killing nine people in 1969. They are believed to have killed many more.

Richard Speck (1941-1991): Richard Speck's father died of a heart attack when Richard was six years old. His mother remarried. His new stepfather came with a criminal record. He was an alcoholic, and the children suffered abuse from him.

Richard Speck's arrests for various crimes began at the age of 13. As an adult, he is believed to have committed a number of murders for which he was never caught. Finally, he was convicted of murdering eight student nurses one night in 1966.

Ted Bundy (1946-1989): Born at a home for unwed mothers, his father's real identity was never confirmed. Bundy murdered over thirty girls and young women from 1974 to 1978.

Pedro Alonzo Lopez (1948 – unknown): Pedro Lopez was one of 13 children born to a Colombian prostitute. He never knew his father. When he was just eight years old, his mother permanently kicked him out of the house. Pedro Lopez became a serial killer, murdering over 350 children. He was known as the Monster of the Andes.

. . .

Stephen Paddock (1953-2017): Among numerous other crimes, Stephen's father, Benjamin Paddock (1926-1998), was convicted of bank robbery. From 1969 to 1977, his father had been on the FBI's most-wanted list. He was arrested when his son, Stephen, was seven years old. Beyond that, he did not spend much time with his son.

The damage of fatherlessness lasts throughout the lives of children, not just when children are growing up. We have seen this multiple times, even in the stories of the Cartainos.

On the night of October 1, 2017, Stephen Paddock killed 60 people as he fired into a country music concert from a Las Vegas hotel across the street. Hundreds more people were wounded. He fired over 1,000 rounds of ammunition. Stephen Paddock then committed suicide. He was 69 years old.

Paddock made a lot of money in his life but lost much of it in his later years. A doctor reportedly described Paddock as having "little emotion." It was later suggested that he may have had an emotional disorder which would have reflected the doctor's observation. He was an atheist who was reported by his girlfriend to be irritated by certain religious practices.

At the time of this writing, the Las Vegas shooting is still the deadliest mass shooting by a single shooter in American history.

Adam Lanza (1992-2012): Adam Lanza's father left when his son was 16 years old. On December 14, 2012, Lanza shot his mother in her home, then killed 20 first-graders and six adults at Sandy Hook Elementary School in Connecticut.

Although Adam Lanza's father was with him when he was young, his mother described his father as "a workaholic." During the week, he left the house early and came back late, often not seeing his children during the week at all.[10]

His father tried to see his children on weekends. In many families, fathers may have legitimate reasons that limit a father's time with his children to weekends. However, even though there might be legitimate reasons, they aren't necessarily enough for some children.

Even when a father should bear no personal blame due to the requirements of making a living, as one example, it doesn't change a child's need for his fathering. Having said that, lots of children turn out fine who also have busy, but otherwise good fathers.

This is why I'm clear that fatherless sons are *not* doomed to be killers. The vast number of fatherless sons are not. However, killers themselves are commonly fatherless.

Even when a father might seem to have been with his children until they were in their teenage years, does not mean that he was *actually with* his children, providing consistent or, in many other cases, *any* fathering. This can be found in any list of fatherless sons. Even if a father was with them, but left before a child reached adulthood, that still leaves a child fatherless.

Recall that Lenin's father left him just one year earlier than Adam Lanza's father left him. Lenin's behavior reportedly changed significantly, for the worse, after that. I say that not to compare Lenin and Lanza. They are obviously quite different. I bring that up as a reminder that, even at 15 or 16 years of age, children still need good fathering. If a father leaves even then, a child becomes fatherless regardless of what had happened before.

Although Adam Lanza's father may have been better than others before he left — and while we cannot make a definitive judgment here — it seems clear that his son needed more. His very involved mother, whom he later killed, was not enough.

In Adam Lanza's case, there were apparently significant mental health issues. Should those have been addressed more effectively had his father been aware of them and still around to provide consistent and involved fathering? We can't know.

All we do know is that, once again, another killer of innocent children and adults, including his own mother, did not have consistent fathering into adulthood.

· · ·

Nikolas Cruz (1998–): Nikolas Cruz was adopted at birth. His birth mother was described as a "horrible mother" with a lengthy criminal record. She abused drugs and alcohol while she was pregnant with him. That's a serious problem that hurts countless children throughout the country today.

Nikolas never knew his birth father.

To make things worse, his adoptive father died in 2004, when Cruz was still very young. His adoptive mother would die not long before the school shootings took place.

Nikolas Cruz had attended Stoneman Douglas High School in Parkland, Florida. The school had expelled him for making threats and for other serious behavioral problems.

On February 14, 2018, and at 19 years of age, Nikolas Cruz went to the high school and shot 34 people, 17 of whom were killed. Three of those who died were school staff who were trying to help and protect students. The students who died were between 14 and 18 years of age. Nikolas Cruz was diagnosed with mental health issues for which he had previously been treated. He was reportedly not receiving treatment at the time of the shootings.

Nonetheless, in the complexity of his problems can also be seen the emotional, behavioral problems, and damage that are frequently associated with fatherlessness. So, one can't pin the problem on mental health issues alone.

At his trial in October 2022, Cruz's public defender reportedly said that he was "doomed from the womb." In actuality, it was his victims who were doomed from that earliest moment. How many others are waiting as their own killers are born today?

Can we not identify those who might be at risk of eventually taking the lives of so many others? Can we not work to change their futures far earlier than is happening today? So far, we aren't doing anything effective at all. In fact, most will say that it isn't even possible. Should this not be among our highest priorities?

People are not born to be killers. All people have value when they are born, really even before. All can grow into valued people who can bring good to the world. Why do some not? We must stop throwing out euphemisms and unhelpful words which only dismiss possible signs of potential future problems as we move on to discuss something else.

On November 2, 2022, Nicholas Cruz was sentenced to life in prison. Families of those he murdered were sad and angry over his sentence.

One last example, among countless others:

Salvador Ramos (2004–2022): On May 24, 2022, Ramos, an 18-year-old gunman, shot and killed 19 elementary school children and two teachers in Uvalde, Texas, as well as injuring a number of others. Ramos had a troubled relationship with his mother. He was living with his grandmother at the time. Before going to the school, he shot his grandmother in the face. As were the others listed here, he was fatherless.

During an early interview after the shooting, his father said that he hadn't spent much time with his son and was often out of the area working anyway. His father reportedly also said, *"My mom tells me he probably would have shot me, too, because he would always say I didn't love him."*[11]

Not feeling loved, whether true or not, is a very serious issue for all children as they grow up. Would the shootings not have occurred had Salvador Ramos believed that he was actually loved by his father? Had his father been with him, raising him with care, would any of this have happened? It's not a stretch to suggest that it would have been far more likely that it wouldn't have happened at all.

✳✳✳

Is the lack of fathers here just so many coincidences? Or is it part of a pattern? Certainly, there must be other causes, too, people add. Yet, even when there are, fatherlessness enters into every one of these killers' lives. Every one.

Can the consistency of this actually be mere coincidence?

When we see violence even at levels far, far below what is seen here, it may be a flag that we may be looking at a fatherless son.

Some people bemoan that interventions were not used before these tragedies happened. Although not in every case, good involved fathers themselves can sometimes be those interventions. Many times, the presence of strong, competent, and loving fathers can either eliminate the need for interventions or support obtaining help when it is clearly needed.

Some feel that schools themselves should be intervening. But they are not mental health facilities. That is not their job and they're not necessarily good at it.

For more on schools, see the book, *Education Is Dead,* also by the author.

The times, cultures, and societies of some other countries are much different from America today. But we cannot help but note the consistent lack of good — or any — fathers raising some of history's most lethal people.

Regardless of culture, we must ask ourselves what would have happened if each person listed above had been brought up by a *good* father? How many lives might have been saved? Shouldn't we be taking the problem of absent and low-quality fathers more seriously?

Indeed, it's possible that most (though perhaps not all) of the fatherless sons listed in this section might have been put on a different path had they been raised in a functional family with both parents present, including a father who loved and properly parented his children. It might not work in every case, but it would certainly have been far more likely.

Society is constantly concerned about violence. Guns often get the blame, even though countries that ban guns still suffer from violence. But even violence isn't actually the problem. It's a *symptom* of the problem. And guns are simply a *tool* used as part of that violence (as are knives, and other weapons). But, regardless of the tools, *one of the foundational causes of violence itself is fatherlessness.*

Recall what John Sowers said earlier, *"The most reliable predictor for gang activity and youth violence is... fatherlessness."*[12]

In spite of regular paltry acknowledgments of the problem, nothing effective is being done to address the problem on a widespread basis. Some think that nothing *can* be done. Some point to children raised with fathers who become violent anyway and, therefore, skip over the problem as not being the real issue.

Some point to poverty (or something else) as the root cause of violence. While it's true that other things can affect the presence of violence, many don't realize that studies show that families with good fathers present, show *less* poverty overall than those without fathers. Like violence, poverty is sometimes a *symptom* of fatherlessness in families.

That's not to say that families with fathers actively present don't also struggle with finances. But, on balance, things are generally not quite as bad when compared to families without competent fathers present at all.

Regardless of anything else, a major, bottom line *cause* of violence and other problems in society *is* fatherlessness. Simply addressing the later problems (the symptoms) caused by fatherlessness won't fix things.

Life is complicated. Fathers (and mothers) are not responsible for all the bad things that happen in the world. They're not responsible for all the bad people. But they're responsible for some, maybe even for many.

Some parents themselves need help to learn how to be good parents. Such help is frequently not available. However, even when it is, it can sometimes include questionable advice, even when such advice comes from certain "professionals."

Studies clearly tell us that we need to take this issue seriously — and we're not doing it.

****

Mothers, in the absence of safety and other serious issues, do all that you can to help your children's father stay with them *from the earliest days* of life until adulthood.

Fathers, do all that *you* can, not only to be with your children, but to be a *good and involved father* when you're with them. You'll never know whose lives you might save because you did.

---

1. Ben Carson's inspirational story, *Gifted Hands* (1996), is worthwhile reading. It is also available as a documentary and as a 2009 movie, *Gifted Hands: The Ben Carson Story*.
2. For another resource with additional information about the specific impacts on sons, see *The Boy Crisis: Why Our Boys Are Struggling and What We Can Do About It* by Warren Farrell, Ph.D. and John Gray, Ph.D. (BenBella Books; 2018).
3. For the full story, see: *Young Stalin*, by Simon Sebag Montefiore (First Vintage Books; 2007). It's a good book if you wish to learn about Stalin's early life.
4. As per: *Stalin's Genocides*, by Norman Naimark (Princeton University Press; 2010).
5. While separated from his wife and son, Stalin's father, on his own, took his son out of school. He then took him to work with him to teach him his craft as a shoemaker. By then, Stalin had no interest in shoemaking. With help, Stalin's mother eventually took him back from his father and put him back in school. Stalin's development during the time he spent in school became a significant foundation that later saw him become part of Vladimir Lenin's revolutionaries. His time in school may have contributed to what would happen in his later life. Today, it might not surprise some that schools can so negatively affect the direction some students can take in life.
6. As per: *worldhistory.org/Attila_the_Hun*, accessed 2-25-2023.
7. As per: *biography.com/political-figures/attila-the-hun*, accessed 2-25-2023.
8. See the book, *Mao: The Unknown Story* (2011) by Jung Chang and Jon Halliday. There are also other sources. Note that books critical of Mao are often themselves criticized seemingly in an effort to defend the legacy of Chairman Mao. Regardless, there are enough sources to confirm the terrors that took place under Mao Zedong.
9. Accurate data on Fidel Castro's childhood isn't widely available. Conflicts exist on that time in his life. "Facts" are often inaccurate. See the book, *Fidel*

Castro's Childhood by Steven Walker (2012; Troubador Publishing, Ltd.) for more information. In spite of what appear to be particular author biases — most authors have them — the book has both substantive information and informed speculation about Castro's early years.

10. See *From a Taller Tower: The Rise of the American Mass Shooter* (2021) by Seamus McGraw.

11. As per an article by Jack Phillips of May 27, 2022, in *The Epoch Times*.

12. See: *Fatherless Generation: Redeeming the Story,* by John A. Sowers. (Zondervan; 2010).

CHAPTER EIGHT
Fatherhood and Marriage

Marriage involves a commitment between two people... whether or not it works out in the end. A couple — often one of them more strongly than the other — will argue that such a formal commitment "isn't necessary." They say that a couple can be committed to each other even without "a piece of paper." Multiple studies show that such thinking is often incorrect.[1]

Of course, many people today don't even understand what a commitment is, let alone be strong enough to keep one.

Issues with marriage are closely entwined with those of fatherlessness.

Among many, marriage today is considered to be just one of multiple equally valid options. Some even believe that marriage is a strongly negative choice feeling that other options are preferable.

For those people, the author recommends the book, *The Case for Marriage: Why Married People Are Happier, Healthier and Better Off Financially,* by Linda Waite and Maggie Gallagher. It makes a strong case that marriage is not only important to the family and the individuals in it, but that it is an essential component of a healthy society. The book's data contrasting marriage with non-marriage options will be enlightening for many.

In light of the arguments put forth by Linda Waite and Maggie Gallagher, the continuing trends confirmed by Gallup and other polls bode poorly for people, and for society in general.

One can argue that, without marriage, it is likely that an out-of-wedlock child will eventually be fatherless, even if a father is around after the baby is born. Multiple studies already bear that out.

There are always some cases when marriage might not be possible or even desirable. But numerous studies show that marriage does far more to keep families together then do non-marriage alternatives. You are again referred to the convincing case made in Linda Waite's book, *The Case for Marriage.*

Many still assume that fathers are the main problem in uncommitted relationships. Yet, in far more cases than many people think, it is the woman who chooses not to be "tied down" in a committed marital relationship. Perhaps she has legitimate concerns about being with the father of her child. Living without a marital commitment is often a couple's shared decision. Many have grown up with a moral compass much different from past generations.

The choices they make will have long term consequences in the lives of their children and for themselves. They should fully understand those options before making their choice.

***

A positive and respectful relationship between a father and mother who are married (and together) is more than just an important example for their children. Parents should remember that children live only temporarily with them. Even though many now live with their parents years longer than in the past, when they do leave home, parents will only have each other left. To prepare for that time, parents need to actively nurture their friendship and caring for each other.

What happens when parents' relationships appear to fall apart? Things should proceed carefully. Sadly, even salvageable relationships are often allowed to die.

That point is well-made in *The Case For Marriage.* Yes, I'm pushing the book.

. . .

***

Quoting government statistics from the National Center for Health Statistics, an April 29, 2020, article in *The Wall Street Journal* reported that *"the U.S. marriage rate fell 6% in 2018, with 6.5 new unions formed for every 1,000 people."*[2]

According to Sally Curtin, lead author of the report, that rate was "the lowest rate since the federal government began keeping data in 1867."

Although "there was no clear reason for the sharp marriage decline in 2018," the article said that difficulties with finances was "a top reason." It mentioned "declining religious adherence" as another cause.

---

1. See: *The Case for Marriage: Why Married People Are Happier, Healthier and Better Off Financially* (2001), by Linda Waite and Maggie Gallagher.
2. See: *The Wall Street Journal,* "U.S. Marriage Rate Plunges to Lowest Level on Record" by Janet Adamy, April 29, 2020.

This section is abridged from:
THE CARTAINOS.

CHAPTER NINE
Forgiveness

Anyone who has been around fatherless daughters, in particular, and spoken to them about this, will realize that the connection with their fathers can be strong and lasting. Their desire for a healthy connection to their father, even a missing father, appears to be innate within them. The longing for their absent father can stay with fatherless daughters throughout their lives, even in those who have tried to bury the loss of their father deeply within them.

That loss is often felt by fathers, too.

Countless biological fathers who are not with their children care deeply about them — even though their children may not always believe it. These men go through their lives covering up a constant hurt, their purported failing (even when the fault is not entirely theirs), and tears that are forever inside them. They distract themselves with other things in life. As they move on in life, most rarely talk about it.

Many men are in constant pain living away from their children. Many still miss their former spouses. Most men want the same things as many women: children, a loving spouse, a family. Where love has not died, an ongoing love for a former spouse only adds to a man's hurt.

In bitter divorces, men can harbor a fear of what the custodial mother of their children might do with the children. That can include intentionally trying to damage children's relationships with their fathers.

Because many men still have a love for their former spouses, they often hope to avoid further damage to the love that may be left between them. Therefore, some may be cautious in how they push back. They do so because, in both men and women, love can quietly continue throughout one or both of their lives.

Although many try to pull a curtain over that part of their lives often by trying not to think about it, it is often a futile attempt to protect themselves from the hurt about which they can do nothing. Others express their loss and frustration in ways they should not.

Some men wrongly take it out on themselves or on others, including their former spouse and children. Those whose lives entwine with these men, have no idea from where their hard words and difficult behaviors may come. Men don't always know either.

Even while still living at home with their children and their children's mother, some fathers quietly withdraw from their role as a father and a husband. Perhaps it begins after repeatedly feeling a rejection of their love or a demeaning of what should be their responsibilities as fathers, assuming they choose to exercise those responsibilities.

True or not, fathers may feel that they do not have the respect of their children or of their wives. Some then lose respect for themselves. These feelings may be expressed in moments of frustration and anger, or sadness and depression.

For whatever reason it happens, low-quality fathering is often the result. This, too, damages children.

***

It is difficult for those who are not suffering to understand all of this. One online reviewer of a book on fathers posted a compelling description of the suffering of many fathers. After giving some background,[1] the reviewer laments that the book's author had not discussed the "madness" inside of many fathers. Poignantly, he goes on to talk about the great sorrow of that "madness."

[It is] not insanity, just a mute madness as you lose your child. Lose your child to his mother, to his stepfather, to his new siblings, to his much more frequent family. The madness of being unnecessary and unneeded. The madness that comes with the realization that your child sees you as a burden that must be endured until the age of 18.

The madness that endures.[2]

***

Let me say this yet another way. Children need *both* parents: a mother and a father. But no parent is perfect.

Too many children deflect blame and criticize others for whatever they don't like or have wrongly done themselves — including blaming their own parents. They may show no patience, no understanding, and no forgiveness.

Of course, *"They're just children."*

Too often that one phrase is used to justify wrong actions of children, especially older children, while condemning potentially correct actions of parents.

Although it can be very difficult, forgiveness and mercy are important parts of healthy souls — but they're often missing. They're rarely even taught as important virtues today. Indeed, the opposite may be happening.

Here is a special call to take better care of fathers, in particular. It's a call to try to bring alienated or separated fathers back into children's lives.

Too many readers are likely to reflexively give examples as to why that won't work, why some fathers should not be back, or why some relationships are unsalvageable. Of course, that is clearly true for some. Too often, it's just an excuse.

Such expressed hopelessness is why so little progress is seen in trying to reclaim fathers among the many good men who genuinely miss their children.

Many women, especially as adults, reach a point where they can tell people that they long ago came to terms with their missing father. Some even write books on it. They might tell people with confidence that they are finally "okay."

But few are. They have just become better at covering up their loss and their hurt, pushing it so deep within them that they hope to no longer know it is there.

In reality, the sadness, anger, confusion, and interior tears brought on by not having been brought up with their father may never really heal in many older, adult children.

Even with outside "professional" help, it can be difficult for fatherless children to cope with life without the presence and love of their father.

It is sad for everyone that many children, especially adult children, do not put a priority on reconnecting and learning from their fathers. Other "more important" priorities in their lives take precedence over time regarding their formerly absent fathers.

***

In *Strong Fathers, Strong Daughters: 10 Secrets Every Father Should Know*[3] (2006), author Meg Meeker takes an unapologetically strong and loving look at fathers and the influence fathers have in the lives of their daughters.

Meg Meeker's book may not always be enough to lead to a broader understanding among many people, nor to make the changes that are needed. Nonetheless, many fathers will benefit from the encouragement she offers. In the introduction to her book, she speaks directly to fathers:

Most of you out there are good men...but you are good men who have been derided by a culture that does not care for you, that, in terms of the family, has ridiculed your authority, denied your importance, and tried to fill you with confusion about your role. But I can tell you that fathers change lives, as my father changed mine. You are natural leaders, and your family looks to you for qualities that only fathers have. You were made a man for a reason, and your daughter is looking to you for guidance that she cannot get from her mother.

For most children, an absent father is keenly missed — whether children know it or not.

---

1. That background included seeing his son what would be an average of just four days a month. More is not known from the posting.
2. Posted by C. B. Dyches, Jan 15, 2017. Accessed May 17, 2019.
3. It should be mentioned that many readers feel strongly about Dr. Meg Meeker's book. The significant majority felt it helped them a lot as fathers. It is a highly rated book. Many reviewers highly recommend it to other fathers. However, a strongly vocal minority disagrees both with what she says and how she says it. Most of those negatives do not appear well-founded. Often, they are held by reviewers who didn't even read much of the book. That is too common today. Nonetheless, the author of the book in your hands highly recommends Dr. Meeker's book, specifically to fathers with daughters.

    One nit: As in the case of many books today, Dr. Meeker's first edition mentions technology that is already outdated. It is hard for any author to look too far into the future when forecasting technology. Likely the book in your hands will also suffer from that after not many more years.

This section is abridged from:
THE CARTAINOS
MEN OF PASSION • MEN OF STONE.

CHAPTER TEN
More On Fathers

S olving the issue of fathers leaving their marriages and their children is more than difficult. In today's culture, it is nearly impossible. Only if the will to do it truly exists, can progress be made. Damningly, the cultures and societies of countries today do not seem capable of doing it. Later in the book, we'll consider some suggestions.

Some books and sociologists seem to say that, through a simple choice, fathers can either leave their children or stay with them. Some say that fatherhood is primarily a socially or culturally dictated way of acting. These people suggest that, beyond the moment of conception, there is little or no biological foundation involved in being a father.

Certain birds and other animals mate for life. Males in some species participate in raising their young. This is certainly an indication that fathering is not simply cultural.

One worthwhile article looked at the results of early trauma on young male elephants (PTSD), especially related to the loss of their fathers and of older male elephants.[1] Later in life, these young elephants could exhibit significant violence. Raised by their mothers without male influence can lead to *"an inability to regulate stress-reactive aggressive states."*

The critical role of older males in normal social development was clearly demonstrated when researchers re-introduced older bulls to quell the young males' violence.

It observed that, after the introduction of those older males, hyper-aggression in the young elephants, along with other abnormalities (including hormonal shifts), *ceased.*

***

In *Father Facts, Eighth Edition* (2019; National Fatherhood Initiative), there is this:

> *During the pre-natal and post-natal period, men experience changes in hormone levels and in their brains that have an impact on the fatherhood role, suggesting that nature prepares men to become fathers.*
> –Section IX: What We Know.

Among other things, *Father Facts, Eighth Edition,* goes on to point to changes in the testosterone and oxytocin levels in men during these times. The origins of such changes are less important than the fact that they appear to support the role of a father with his children.

When either men or women work against a healthy hormone, harmful things can happen both to them and to those around them. One might surmise that this is what happens to many men who leave their families.

Fathers may be fighting against the biology within them when they walk away from their children and families. But their walking away does not prove that the innateness of fatherhood does not exist, as some people puzzlingly seem to suggest.

I expect future research will continue to show that fathers do damage to themselves (and others) when they push back in an attempt to ignore the fatherhood within them. More research is needed to address the hypotheses suggested here and elsewhere.[2]

On the other hand, while more serious research is always

important, fathers and families should not wait for it. There is already plenty of evidence that, at least in part, fatherhood has a biological basis.

***

Many times, children blame their father for leaving them, for not being there for them. They may or may not blame their mother. Of course, to children, it's all about them. The world revolves around them. That's understandable. They are just children.

The vast majority of men do not want to leave their children. Although there are many exceptions, they are just that: exceptions. But it is those exceptions that are touted as normative malbehavior for men who "callously" leave their children.

Some "bad fathers" may be wrongly defined as such by a bitter mother, by a changing society, or by others who are not even part of the family.

What causes properly defined "bad fathers" in the first place? Their own upbringing? Too often, they themselves had a bad father at home — or no father at all.

Such a cycle can only be stopped by those actively determined to do so. People must become aware of the issue. Most adults who grew up with a missing or low-quality father don't even know they have been affected by it.

Both genetics and active parenting play significant roles in children's lives. Can we then generalize that good fathers raise good children while bad fathers raise bad ones? Not always. But often we can.

Many consciously overcome the effects of a bad parent to become incredibly fine adults. Others turn to the dark side of life, even when raised by loving parents who are wonderful mentors and role models. Here, I put those aside to look at the bigger picture.

✳✳

In many families, mothers often act to reduce the damage caused by a missing or bad father. Single mothers do difficult and wonderful things raising children on their own. But their success is rarely complete. We all hope their children will truly appreciate their mother's work, her emotional challenges, and her self-sacrifice when the children are adults.

What about stepfathers?

When a divorced or widowed mother with children marries a good man who willingly steps into the role of father, it can be a good thing for all.

Many stepchildren who are brought up in a loving and richly rewarding environment are better off than with some biological fathers. Many well-reared stepchildren will attest to that.

Countless wonderful stepfathers help to sustain loving families. They have been responsible for helping to raise many wonderful people in the world.

Nonetheless, some studies show that abuses are significantly more likely to occur with a stepparent in the family than when both natural parents are together. This can be a serious concern.

Referring to other studies, David Popenoe is clear that both children and their mothers are at significantly higher risk of abuse with a stepfather present than with a biological father in the home.[3]

There is some indication that the best results with stepfathers are more likely to occur when a stepfather steps in while a child is still an infant or young toddler.

We do not want to detract from the many amazing and generous stepparents. However, studies and the experiences of many children tell us that stepparents are not always positive additions to the lives of children.

Of course, vast numbers of children are raised as part of remarkable single-parent families throughout the world. We know that will never end.

Another reality is that countless children today are being raised by social media, by online "connections" to others. It quickly becomes an addiction — not only to children but also to their parents. Many are now convincing that this is not merely unhealthy — it is dangerous.

The increasingly adult themed television programs have also become an ongoing problem for children of all ages. Most parents are unable (or unwilling) to control their children's access. But its importance is such that all must take action very early if people are to protect themselves and their children from the multiple dangers to individuals, families, and society.

Regarding former spouses posing legitimate threats (not merely vindictive accusations), mothers must, of course, be protective of their safety and that of their children.

***

Thoughtful people might realize that men most often leave their wives, not their children. Their children are "collateral damage." Their fathers don't want that to happen, but it is often a consequence of a marriage not working out. That's why marriage itself is so important here.[4]

For a convincing discussion of this, read *The Case for Marriage: Why Married People Are Happier, Healthier and Better Off Financially* by Linda Waite and Maggie Gallagher (Broadway Books; 2000, 2001). Some data may seem slightly dated, but the conclusions are just as valid today, if not more so. It is recommended reading.

***

When talking about absent fathers and their children, there is the assumption that we are only talking about *children*. We are not.

Those "children" grow up. The damage done to children carries on far into adulthood. So we have generation after generation of damaged adults, of sad adults, of depressed adults, of violent adults, of promiscuous adults, of adults who have taken their own lives, of adults without a traditional code of morality. Yet children — whether adult or younger — rarely know what has led them on these paths.

***

David Popenoe summarizes all of this succinctly:

"The repercussions [of fatherlessness] go far beyond children to include a steady deterioration in the lives of adult men and women. If present trends continue, our society could be on the verge of committing social suicide.[5]*"*

***

Later in the book, we will consider suggestions on what might be done about all this.

[Note that a short Digression in *The Cartainos: Men of Passion • Men of Stone* called, *More About Parenting*, is not included in this book. That Digression offers an additional discussion on parenting.]

---

1. See: *Nature* 433, 807 (Feb 24, 2005). CONCEPTS, *Elephant breakdown*, by G. A. BRADSHAW, ALLAN N. SCHORE, JANINE L. BROWN, JOYCE H. POOLE & CYNTHIA J. MOSS found at: elephants.com/pdf/PTSD.pdf, accessed Jan 7, 2023.

2. As we have seen in some past research, cultural and sociological assumptions and biases which find their way into some research designs risk returning results that are misleading and, therefore, unhelpful. Competent future research should be designed both with and without social and cultural biases.

3. See *Families Without Fathers: Fatherhood, Marriage and Children in American Society* by David Popenoe (2009).

4. Research shows that *un*married relationships with children involved are much more likely to fail than married ones.

5. As per David Popenoe: *Families Without Fathers: Fatherhood, Marriage and Children in American Society*, (Routledge; 2009), pg 192.

Chapter 11

Many Books Ignore the Issue of Fatherlessness

Books discussing school shooters, serial and other killers are generally in agreement that there are multiple complex causes and that we can't identify a single, primary, shared cause among these killers that has led to such great numbers of deaths.

For whatever reason, those studying these mass shooting/mass killing events continue to overlook the most obvious one. It doesn't take years of in-depth studies to see what clearly links the vast majority of these events: bad or missing fathers and dysfunctional families.

Before starting, I have to make the point — yet again — that some bad people can come from really good families and parents. But it doesn't happen often, and I won't be looking at such instances here.

Most importantly, again, the corollary to "Killers Are Fatherless," isn't necessarily true: fatherless (youth) are *not* necessarily killers. Many become truly fine people.

Now, we'll continue.

***

Here is one book's comments on a shooter of years ago:

"There is no obvious indication that the sins of the father were visited on the son. The killer was seven years old when his father was imprisoned and rarely saw him after that."[1]

In this case, the killer's father was a criminal. Do we dismiss his father's influence — or non-influence — as though there was nothing bad going on because his father wasn't there? To do so, unconscionably disregards the damage *an absent father* can cause. It's certainly true that it's best that some bad fathers aren't around their children at all. But that only looks at the possible lesser of two evils.

If a bad father is not with his children (a good thing), it does not eliminate the children's need for a father. Could a stepfather have stepped in? Possibly. There are wonderful stepfathers in the world. However, as we have heard, data show that abuse from some stepfathers happens more frequently than it does from biological fathers.

However, to say that a son might not turn out poorly because a father, who *did* turn out poorly, was not around may not be accurate at all.

The absence of bad does not necessarily ensure the presence of good.

Sons (and daughters) need a father who is with them, who provides good *fathering* as they grow up. To suggest that because a bad father was gone, there will be little chance that his son might later become violent — or a killer — completely disregards the serious damage done to his child by not having a father at all.

Even though it was likely good that this particular bad father was not around, that does not eliminate fatherlessness as the major cause for his son becoming a future killer. Yet, along with too many other books and articles, that particular book seemingly fails to recognize, or at least acknowledge, this issue.

Surely, that book's author must be aware of damage done to fatherless children. Yet the book rarely even mentions fathers of mass shooters.[2]

In partial redemption, that same book offers this insight as he quotes from *The Body Keeps the Score: Brain, Mind, and Body in the Healing of Trauma* (2015) by Bessel van der Kolk M.D.:

> *"'...traumatic experiences do leave traces, whether on a large scale (on our histories and cultures) or close to home, on our families, with dark secrets being imperceptibly passed down through generations.'"*

As we follow multiple generations, we see that damage resulting from the loss of a father, even in prior generations, can indeed be passed down through subsequent generations. Those later generations may have known nothing about that earlier loss at all, nor of the damage it caused. One generation of fatherlessness often leads to others.

As just one example, *The Cartainos: Men of Passion • Men of Stone* describes one family line with *five* generations of fatherless children — and it hadn't ended at the time of its writing.

Are there other complexities that contribute to or exacerbate such violence? Indeed, there are. The multiple contributing complexities discussed by other books and shown in some studies are certainly real. They can appear alone or mixed with others. They are not only seen in the events themselves, but also in the analyses of those events.

In some cases, as with genetically inherited traits of certain mental illnesses, they can appear to be a major cause or a contributing cause of extreme violence.

Other contributing factors may be peer influences (sometimes including pervasive cultures of violence, as with gangs), violent media (which includes a variety of things), bullying, and more.

However, when one looks more broadly at the shared foundation of such things, there is seemingly only one thing that potentially stands out as the major *foundational* cause of these events.

That one thing is the absence of a good father, low-quality fathering, or a dysfunctional family. If that sounds like three separate issues, it's generally just one.

However, there are indeed times when we can separate the fathering issue from a dysfunctional family, especially when one parent — father or mother — is acting irrationally. Regardless, it will have a similar effect on the upbringing of children. These things occur throughout the years the child grows up, even as older teens.

As mentioned more than once, we are defining fatherlessness to be a child growing up without a father — hopefully a biological father — or with low-quality or bad fathering *to adulthood*.

We use that definition because, when we observe children who show signs of fatherlessness, even in later life, that is generally what we see. To say a child is not fatherless because their otherwise good father was with them until their mid to late teens isn't enough. How do we know?

It's because we see so many children who grew up having lost a father — or with a low-quality father — during that especially important time. Many then made predictably poor choices or had difficult lives in what data can predict in fatherless children. It's not there in every case, but it's too consistent to ignore.

✳✳✳

Let's look at another book to see the near absence of serious consideration of the damage of fatherlessness.

In *Rampage, The Social Roots of School Shootings* (2004) by

Katherine S. Newman, et al, we find this next segment. Count how many times the word "father" appears (or doesn't appear):

> *"No explanation for school shootings has received more attention than family problems.* The Final Report of the Congressional Bipartisan Working Group on Youth Violence *is a good example of the notion that it all begins in the home: 'Although there is no single cause for youth violence,' the report concludes, 'the most common factor is family dysfunction.' But what kind of families are these? Here the picture gets murkier. A Secret Service study of forty-one school shooters who committed their crimes between 1974 and 2000 found that the perpetrators come from a variety of backgrounds, ranging 'from intact families with numerous ties to the community to foster homes with histories of neglect.'*
>
> *Problems within the family such as divorce, domestic or sexual abuse, frequent relocations, and fragile family relationships as well as a lack of awareness or involvement in children's lives were all cited by people we interviewed...as reasons that youths turn violent."*

The book goes on to mention a seventh-grade teacher who *"was convinced that the home and family are the root of the problem."*

The seventh-grade teacher was right. What is not right is the reliance on those things in the list of family failings in the last paragraph quoted above. Too many authors and researchers appear to consistently judge a functional or dysfunctional family based on the presence or absence of those or a limited number of other traits.

The problem is this. Even in a family where *"divorce, domestic or sexual abuse, frequent relocations, and fragile family relationships as well a lack of awareness or involvement in children's lives"* isn't present, we don't necessarily see good fathering, or good parenting generally.

Although to some it might appear otherwise, as I have repeatedly said, the absence of bad things in a family does not necessarily mean the presence of good things, such as good fathering.

Therefore, we are not looking for the absence of bad things, but for the presence of good things that are critical in the development of children. Often, that is hard to judge and even to observe. It can be hard to ascertain by just talking to parents, and even talking to some children.

Yet books look at the absence of those bad things and immediately assume a killer's home life had not been a problem. They then move on to talk about mental health or guns.

That is often a major mistake.

Later in that same book, however, we do find this observation:

"Did school shooters tend to have serious family problems? The Secret Service researchers found scant evidence of family problems, in part because they limited their analysis to living arrangements, in which few patterns emerge. Nearly two-thirds of the shooters [in this book's limited numbers] lived in two-parent families. This is not what criminologists have come to expect...; they have in mind single-parent families. Clearly, however, family structure is not the key variable in school shootings. The quality of family life — the extent to which parents get along with one another, the degree to which they express excessive or harsh disapproval of their sons... may be much more important than whether there are two of them in the house."

That is a critical observation because looking at family structure alone is one way that other authors and researchers determine whether a violent child's home life had anything to do with the violence we would see in them later on.

Newman (the author) does go on to say:

"Eighty-five percent of the shooters in our database were said to come from dysfunctional homes, were suicidal or depressed, or suffered from a major mental illness."

Admittedly, dysfunctional families, sometimes separate from issues of fatherlessness, can cause great destruction by themselves.

By the way, did you see the word "father" in any of those recently three quoted sections that were just evaluated here? I didn't.

I don't mean to be specifically picking on this or any other book quoted here. These books are truly just examples of the seemingly widespread neglect of this issue. Many books neglect it.

Authors and researchers frequently analyze shootings looking from the end back. Yet if we look from the beginning forward, we often see something entirely different.

***

The book, *Why Kids Kill: Inside the Minds of School Shooters* (2009) by Peter Langman, Ph.D., does a better job than many in addressing the connection of families to school shooters. However, the separate and crucial role of fathers is not discussed.

More than once, we hear or read things that purport to contain the sum total of what is good or bad in a family.

As one example, when discussing two school shooters, we're told that they *"came from stable homes without abuse, parental alcoholism, or other significant problems."* The book notes that these two particular shooters came from *"more harmonious families"* than others, although they had serious mental health issues.

Having said all that, that author moves on as if he had now put to rest concerns about the shooters' families.

Nothing to see here. Move along.

Elsewhere, we read that, like those two shooters with apparently good families, a different shooter *"came from a family with*

an intact marriage and no known violence or abuse of any kind."
This shooter's parents were *"so opposed to weapons that... they did
not even let him play with toy guns"* when he was little.

"Intact" families do not necessarily mean that parents are
providing correct parenting.[3] That is too often noted in such a way
as to allow an author or researcher to dismiss the family as a foundational cause for violent children (especially sons).

Later still, we read about other school shooters. These others:

*"...came from families where there was no known abuse, neglect,
parental alcoholism, or parental incarceration. Outwardly, at
least, there were no significant problems."*

That comment does leave open that perhaps the seeming lack of
problems might just be external and that there could be some
unseen problems. It's not enough for a judgment to be made.

However, in spite of substantive past data on the possibility,
the book seems to assume there likely aren't any family concerns.
Fathers aren't mentioned. Am I misunderstanding something?

Really, families and fathers of the shooters mentioned may
indeed be solid and superlative. A full understanding of this is
difficult. Yet the stance of most outside observers is that, if there is
no definitive evidence of fatherlessness or a bad family life, all is
well. However, that ignores substantive evidence to the contrary
when looking at violent youth.

Internal dynamics within families is sometimes all but
unknowable, regardless of what outside observers might conclude.
But, in many other cases, it really isn't difficult to know at all.

The openness of that author that something unknown might
still be present is good. But, as repeatedly noted, the absence of
bad things at home does not mean the presence of good things,
such as strong and effective parenting and, especially, fathering.

———————————

1. *As per,* From a Taller Tower: The Rise of the American Mass Shooter (2021) *by Seamus McGraw. There is good history in this book. But it is a serious omission in not suggesting that fatherlessness may be a significant cause of violence in many children — especially in sons — and that mass shooters are often from such backgrounds. Sadly, even in the face of many statistics pointing to the damage of fatherlessness as well as the compelling partial, list of killers in this book, many other books also fail to take this seriously into account.*
2. *See:* From a Taller Tower: The Rise of the American Mass Shooter (2021) *by Seamus McGraw.*
3. *Note that good or correct parenting is not defined here. It is difficult to define and will always be debated. Although it is addressed in* The Cartainos, *including in a Digression in the book, it would be a book in itself if it is to be adequately discussed. Even then, we're unlikely to come up with a definition all can accept.*

Chapter 12

Parents Should Watch Over Their Children

Reading about killers and fatherlessness can be disconcerting. So it's important to keep things in perspective. Looking at the bigger picture, the percentage of children who kill — whether as children or as adults — is very small. This is another reminder that fatherless children can and do grow up to be wonderful people. They can be remarkably successful in their lives.

But the ones who don't are serious and must be addressed.

***

It's great that families can appear harmonious and that both parents remain together. That can be a wonderful foundation in which to raise wonderful children. Too many families don't have that today. But direct, positive, loving, structured parenting, and especially fathering, is also required.

Defining good and effective parenting — other than love and communication generally — would be a separate book.

The main intent here is to call attention to the connection of killers to fatherlessness. That is done both by looking at the fatherless statistics, but also by looking at the extensive earlier list of fatherless killers over the centuries. Does anything else connect such a diverse list other than fatherlessness? There are no other links that we can see. Even were there others, fatherlessness would remain as a connecting link regardless.

Parents should take note when something potentially serious appears. Children can appear happy early on. But children can change. Such changes sometimes go unnoticed by parents.

Avoiding that can only happen by closely monitoring children as well as loving and frequent interactions with them, including effective corrections when needed for wrong behaviors. One would think all that should be obvious. However, we should assume nothing when it comes to raising our children.

The issue of mental illness bears another mention. Schizophrenia and other mental illnesses can, to various extents, be inherited. Sometimes, resulting behaviors might feel as though they're beyond the control of anyone. When needed, parents should involve mental health professionals. Even some really good families can have a history of mental illness. This is another reason why having a full health history in families is so important.

Blame for killings sometimes seems to be put on mental illness just because of the violence itself, without actually knowing whether or not such illness was actually present at the time.

Again, I'm not a mental health professional. Nothing in this book should be considered to be professional advice. Call a real mental healthcare professional for accurate advice.

In some cases, school shooters left behind journals of their feelings and thinking that should have been troubling enough to lead any parent or teacher to take action to address what they saw. Troubling writings can be openly found in yearbooks or in school writing assignments. Why aren't parents seeing these things — and taking them seriously? Do they not review schoolwork, even with older children? Do they not continue to take an active interest in what is happening with their children at school, online, and else-where — including in their bedrooms?

Too many don't.

Children try to reassure parents about clearly troubled writings that teachers or parents see. It's almost always unwise for parents or teachers to brush off such writings as not being of concern. Instead, such writings should minimally be a call for an immediate talk with the child and for a deeper look into what is going on.

Although a child may be totally innocent of something or parents might be misinterpreting something, it's important to err on the side of taking such writings seriously and act accordingly.

Any time something of serious concern is noted, action to address those concerns must be undertaken. That doesn't always mean addressing it directly with their child, although it often does. Instead, and especially when something might be of special danger or concern, it should involve getting outside advice and help.

However, there are indeed times when even the best parents may have no idea that some overwhelming sludge of life has been growing in their child who may become confused, depressed, or angry. Such may then allow an inner anger or depression to fester and grow. Finally, it can all explode inside of them.

Children can be very good at hiding things from parents. Parents must be equally good at quietly finding such hidden things to ensure that their child, and possibly others, remain safe.

If a child's friends or others at school express concerns, they should be taken seriously even if you later find there was no cause for concern.

Times when such things seem to come out of nowhere should be rare. In most cases, there are signs that parents or others miss or ignore before something finally happens. When children get in trouble at school, too many parents blame the school — teachers, administrators, other students — rather than taking it as a concerning flag that something serious might be wrong. There might indeed be nothing wrong, but parents should explore these things and be sure about their judgments, if that's even possible.

✳✳✳

I condemn the frequent thinking that if bad things in a family aren't happening — or aren't seen — then bad fathering and bad parenting have no bearing on any later violence or deaths. Parents should be treating their children with love and caring while carefully watching over them.

Foundational to everything is love and caring for children. However, love and caring doesn't mean fully trusting children, thinking that they're basically good and will get over something serious on their own. They're growing and need their parents to guide them. As we all did growing up, they'll be making mistakes, hopefully, but not always, little ones.

That thinking is often there because so many studies only study the presence or absence of certain measurable behaviors. Some things simply aren't easy to measure. So they're left out. But those unmeasurables might, in fact, be part of the foundational causes of later violence or other bad behaviors in children.

As said before, it will always be difficult or impossible to know the extent of the presence or absence of good parenting. Parents don't necessarily self-report mistakes they've made or, if they do, they're might be minor.

Children may wrongly report things they don't like that their parents do to them. Perhaps they wrongly think a parent made them feel bad and that no one should ever make them "feel bad." Perhaps they complain for some other reason. Yet such complaints might actually fall within the realm of good parenting, however that is defined at any particular moment. Indeed, the definition of "good parenting" is often in the eye of the beholder. There are few universally accepted definitions.[1]

Then there is the more recent and serious issue of both government and other people wrongly defining appropriate and effective parenting — including necessary discipline — as "abuse." Often such "abuse" is defined today as including almost anything that makes a child "feel bad" or sets unwelcome boundaries of behaviors for the child.

Parental concern about that can be a problem in raising children. It can take effective and necessary parenting out of the hands of parents. This has become a serious issue in recent times and needs to be fixed. (Actual abuse is a different matter.)

Of course, there truly are some terrible parents. Sometimes parents have their own serious mental illnesses, yet are tasked with providing parenting for their children.

Nonetheless, be careful assigning blame. Sometimes things are beyond the wisdom of anyone.

This can all be terribly difficult.

On the other hand, sometimes, it's not.

School shooters don't just kill other students and school staff. Too often, they shoot their parents first, even ones they love. So, it's wise to take the upbringing of children seriously. Love doesn't mean letting children get by with things that won't contribute to their becoming a good and loving adult. But it should still remain the core of all that a parent is.

If help is needed, parents might also consider joining parenting support groups. Parenting classes might also be available, although those teaching some of those classes should be evaluated with care.

✳✳✳

Just how pervasive is all this? It's far more prevalent than people know.

Sometimes, we can look back and see where an adjustment in fathering or parenting may have made a life-changing difference.

It's clearly better to look forward — before a life-taking event occurs — rather than to look back after it's already too late.

Can we say that the number of violent children and violent adults would be reduced if all were raised with good fathering as part of strong and healthy families?

Yes. We can almost assuredly make that claim.

---

1. Note that good or correct parenting is not defined here. It will always be debated. Although it is addressed in a Digression in *The Cartainos*, it would be a book in itself to be adequately addressed. Fortunately, plenty of books are already available.

Chapter 13

We Must All Stop Ignoring Fatherlessness

I repeat what was said earlier: Just because children come from a fatherless or single parent family does *not* mean they will become bad or violent people. The vast number of such children do not. It's the reverse question that we must consider: Have violent people generally come from a fatherless or dysfunctional family? In most cases, we seem to find that the answer is yes. Are those from fatherless or dysfunctional families *destined* to become violent or bad people? In most cases, we'll find that answer is no.

Although children often beg their fathers to father them — neither those children nor their fathers might even know it. It is sometimes a silent plea as children grow. Children don't know they're asking — because they don't even know what they're asking for.

We must listen closely through the silence to know what must be done. The responsibility to grow up well is not on young children. It's on their parents, both their father and their mother. Secondarily, it's on the community — on the rest of us.

However, we all *do* know that our children ask for love. They always ask for love. (So do adults.)

But, in other cases, children are not silent. Many children actively call out for their father. Silent or aloud, that call must be heeded.

Those who insist on nit-picking the numbers as to whether or not a father (*any* father) was present in a particular killer's home as they were growing up, appear to be going out of their way to suggest that absent fathers aren't really the enormous problem we can all see in the data. Beyond the data, others have observed this for countless years.

When such naysayers try to tear down this national calamity by attacking lesser issues surrounding the main problem, they actively work against strengthening families, fathering, and a wider acknowledgment of this critical problem.

Here is one example of those actively working against children being raised by a married father and mother. Such people's attitudes directly contribute to fatherlessness.

Some comments by the Family Heritage Alliance had directly referenced the federal *Fourth National Incidence Study of Child Abuse and Neglect* (NIS–4). That report referred to data stating that the safest place for children is in a family with a married father and mother.

Unfathomably, one elected Democratic state representative strongly objected to that. Despite substantive evidence to the contrary, on February 13, 2023, this representative tweeted:

> "Extremist group Family Heritage Alliance said this morning that the safest place for kids are in families that have a married mom and dad. *What a dangerous and un-American belief* [emphasis added]." — South Dakota Democratic State Representative Erin Healy[1]

Even from that one example, we see that there really are those who work in support of *perpetuating* fatherlessness. Others still insist that concerns over fatherlessness are overblown — that there are alternatives — their own agenda-rich alternatives. With an awareness of the existence of those who attack families and fathers, you might now more easily see it when it happens.

As another example, see an article appearing in *The Washington Post* on January 10, 2017: "The Dangerous Myth Of The 'Missing Black Father'." Preferring to blame racism, the article's subtitle tells us, "Responsible fatherhood only goes so far in a world plagued by institutionalized oppression."

We also read about "the *supposed* absence of black fathers." (Emphasis added.) *Supposed absence?*

The data has been massive and consistent as to the pervasiveness of fatherlessness in the Black community, yet the article's title calls it merely a "myth." For countless years, leaders in the Black community itself have strongly called attention to the problem.

At other times, the article appears to suggest that fatherlessness exists primarily only in the Black community. Although the problem is especially severe there, it affects all peoples everywhere.

All should make immediate and aggressive moves to solve this — or at least make it substantially better than it is now. Otherwise, the problem will continue to be briefly acknowledged, as it has been, before once again being ignored.

Many naysayers point to just one or two examples where a killer was raised in a two-parent household — supposedly in good families — who went on to be violent anyway. Their insinuation is that since there are ANY exceptions, the whole thesis falls apart. That's faulty logic.

Of course, there are other factors that contribute to killers and other problems of society. I'm not excluding them. There is complexity in most things. But those other factors frequently *follow* a fatherless upbringing. Except in specific cases (genetic inheritance of mental illness, for example), such other factors are rarely, if ever, a foundational cause that will set the stage for later tragedies.

Dysfunctional families, but especially fatherlessness, are not simply one of many causes of killers. They appear to be *the* foundational cause.

If all children were brought up by good fathers would *all* violence and killings stop? Of course, they would not. But the number of deaths would be cut dramatically. Therefore, to fail to aggressively move forward to solve this problem would put the responsibility for future deaths on us. As a byproduct, we would discover we would have both happier children and happier adults.

The issue of guns will be brought up again in a later chapter.

***

What can be done about all this? Complex problems are sometimes so complex as to get ignored in favor of easier messaging.

Especially in early reporting of school or mass shootings, killers' backgrounds are rarely fully known. Therefore, reporting moves on to the events themselves, looking at what is visible while ignoring what is not visible. That, of course, is understandable. People cannot report on that of which they aren't aware.

That earlier book is not alone in its author's frustrations about guns. It represents many other books, writings, caring authors, reporters, first responders, politicians, and regular people who feel the same way.

If one disagrees that fatherlessness and dysfunctional families have any significant bearing on the violence of killing and death, then so be it. Make that case, difficult or impossible as that may be.

But to so fully disregard both the data and its presence in so many killers is, in my opinion, inexcusable.

Damage from fatherlessness does not simply affect young people. It affects people *throughout their entire lives*. It goes well into adulthood, into middle age — even into our advanced years. It affects (almost) everyone brought up fatherless or in dysfunctional families in which violence later emerges. Too many times, it goes on to affect their children — and their children's children.

To discuss any issue of extreme violence, while ignoring what I feel is so frequently its foundational cause, seems to me to border on a malpractice of life.

This is not meant to say that books which relegate fatherlessness to a secondary role in violence — if they acknowledge any role at all — do not have importance. They do.

***

Just because a person of violence is fatherless or from a dysfunctional family does not mean that they should not be removed from society in order to protect others, as well as receive a just punishment.

Fatherlessness may be a reason for the violence, but it is never an *excuse* for violence. Once someone becomes violent, they're violent. That generally means locking them away from society in order to protect others. Today, countless violent people are repeatedly put back on the streets as a result of some failing criminal justice systems in the country. Many have seen repeated reports on that.

However, our efforts must also be to prevent future societal violence due to fatherlessness or dysfunctional families by directly addressing the damage of those issues.

All this might seem impossible to do. But we can't throw up our collective hands and accept this widespread problem as the way things are and always will be. New, aggressive moves to combat this pandemic must be undertaken.

I am personally very concerned at the large numbers of people who are *actually innocent*, or have been given unjust sentences, in prisons today.

However, I am *not* concerned that people of violence are locked away, especially actual or potential killers. And I absolutely do not support using the damage of fatherlessness as an excuse to allow violent people back out on the streets.

Having said all that, our society can make a future difference in stopping children from becoming violent in the first place — or from becoming sad, depressed, or experiencing failed relationship after failed relationship — if we can figure out how to turn around the plague of fatherlessness. It is not likely to be fully possible. But we have to try. Things are already in extremis.

---

1. As per:
    twitter.com/RepErinHealy/status/1625219121687437312, accessed 2-21-2023.

Chapter 14

Response To Objectors And Deniers

In addition to my earlier responses, I spend another few minutes to again address some objectors and deniers. It's appalling to me how many people want to argue against this, in spite of the ongoing supportive data, as noted earlier.

There are those who twist the arguments to say that proponents of the damage of fatherlessness are attacking families headed by mothers or grandmothers, as just two examples. Such twistings are often related to those who demean the separate importance of *fathering* itself, not just parenting more generally.

This book does not discuss single parenting. Of course, that form of parenting is often the natural remnant of a missing father. (Yes, some single parent families are run by fathers. But most are not.) Twisting all this to fit one's separate agenda is another reason nothing is happening to change the situation.

I'm not saying not to study gun violence or anything else. Well-constructed studies often lead to more understandings and often to even more questions for which we'd also like answers.

The problem is the constant studying of things without eventually taking action based on those studies. Whenever a study is done, the next step is... another study! After all, don't we want to consider *all* the countless variables? Those studies then go on for years more. Meanwhile, countless more die while we await results on which no action is taken anyway — except to await the next studies or hearings.

We can't solve all the problems surrounding this, but we're not even making a substantive effort. Isn't there something to be said for common sense? After all the time for these studies, does anyone care anymore? When we already have substantive evidence, studies, and data — as we do now — we need to move forward to address the problem, not wait for even more of which we already have enough.

More studies are good only when action is taken on the outcomes. Actions that must be taken should not be quick, thoughtless actions based on the feelings of the moment. (Some suggest that is a common problem of democracy itself.) If a new study turns up different information later, our actions can be modified. Regardless, action should be taken now — if we can figure out what will work.

Studies should not be an end in themselves. But they often are.

One can always point to things for which hearings and investigations are currently being called. Yet extensive hearings on many of those things were *already* conducted decades earlier! No one remembers them today. Therefore, people assume we just have to start over.

Not only do they not know such hearings/investigations were already done but, even if someone points them out, people will say it's "too old" and that we need to do them again. Later, people will forget about these new ones — *again*. Therefore, no action will be taken — *again*.

✳✳✳

Many politicians continue to say that we need more "gun laws" in order to stop the killings.

But note that we're not outlawing knives or human hands. Those are also used as tools of death — and they're used often.

It's the violence itself that must be addressed, not simply the tools of violence. No violence; no tools needed. I'm not suggesting to completely ignore some of those tools. I'm simply saying that those are not the foundational cause of violence.

It's the gratuitous and societally destructive violence we must address. Violence itself is not an underlying cause. It's a symptom or result of a foundational cause. Eventually, we can't help but get back to fathering, parenting, or some other identifiable cause – such as the genetic inheritance of a mental health issue.

Addressing another misleading objection, we don't solely need to "increase funding to support families" without a targeted, achievable, and measurable goal. That's a carrot some deniers and objectors throw out to those who continue pointing to fatherlessness and dysfunctional families as a major cause of violence.

But such "increased funding" is not good enough. We need a massive and immediate effort to address the problem. The problem is already far too big for a token increase in "funding."

***

A commentary of June 9, 2022 by Jeffery M. Leving in *The Chicago Sun-Times* quotes the statistic that 72% of all teenage murderers grew up without fathers. It says that fatherlessness is *"the most reliable predictor of crime in America."*

But inexplicably, it then goes on to say that *"...when it comes to mass shootings, we still need more evidence to support the theory."*

So let me understand this. "Regular" teenage murderers are somehow *so very different* from mass shooters that we need "more evidence" of a linkage to fatherlessness in *those* other mass shooters?[1] Maybe because they might not be teenagers? I'm clearly confused here.

Exactly why do we not err — and I question whether we're

erring at all — on the side already supported by numerous statistics, moving forward immediately to address the fatherless problem. Simultaneously with taking action, we can certainly conduct additional studies, if needed. It's the additional *waiting* for new and never-ending studies without taking action that we should not accept.

That Chicago Sun-Times article ends by saying that we need to "address and solve this problem immediately." Perhaps we should ask for a definition of "immediately." Three-to-five more years after getting "more evidence?" A decade more because in that three to five year study we discovered more unanswered questions?

My point here is that we should not wait for more studies. The crisis has already been destroying the country — and the world — for too long. There is already enough data available to let us see a connection between fatherlessness and violence, generally. We must proceed *right now* to address this and to address it aggressively.

Turning to fatherless daughters for a moment, we see relatively consistent damage to countless daughters, especially in the relationships they have throughout their lives.

If fatherlessness causes documented damage to daughters as well as documented damage to sons, why would we possibly be surprised that it actually causes even more terrible things?

***

Why are there so many people consistently in denial, often with an agenda to push back against the clarity of fatherlessness as a/the primary cause. Isn't the social decay we already have enough?[2]

It is.

One blogger separates the causes of fatherlessness from each other. For instance, the situation where a father has died is noted as being different from a father who abandons his family. Causes of fatherlessness other than death are also mentioned. So, what is that blogger saying? That children don't grow up fatherless because their father died instead of willfully abandoning them?

So it's okay if a child is fatherless if there's a good reason for it? Regardless of the reason, a child growing up without a father can still suffer the same bad outcomes.

In addition — and depending on the facts of each situation — the mere accusation of fathers "abandoning" children and spouses can unjustly put the blame on innocent fathers for not being with their children. (Of course, some fathers are certainly not blameless.) Nonetheless, fathers generally *do* carry the responsibility for not fathering their children.

---

1. *Note that the definition of mass shooters varies depending on the source. A definition is less important than the fact that lives were lost and, in most cases, it appears that the shooters were fatherless.*
2. *I'm admittedly avoiding the separate LGBTQ talking points which, for obvious reasons, often have separate reasons for not accepting the basic premise here.*

Chapter 15

Some Understandable Reasons For Reduced or Absent Fathering

A re there understandable reasons why a father might not be able to provide the good fathering he knows he should provide? Are there understandable reasons children might not be able to see and be parented by a good and loving father?

Of course, there are. Here are some of them:

1. Financial distress requiring a father to work two or more jobs (as well as actual physical exhaustion from working them). This may result in being unable to be home with their children while they are still awake. (Of course, this applies to mothers, too.);

2. Jobs requiring long absences (i.e.: military deployments, cross country driving work, etc). Other work that requires someone to live too far from family to be able to be present for their children. (Options to

avoid these things should be seriously considered although, sometimes, they're just not possible.);

3. Limited interactions with children due to court restrictions, agreements, or an uncooperative and estranged spouse following a divorce or separation;

4. Single parenting;

5. Debilitating physical or mental illness of the father;

6. Incarceration.

But here's the thing. Even though most of these reasons can indeed mitigate the *blame* for fathers who cannot be with their children, they do not eliminate the fatherless damage they can do to their children. Even though many children will survive and sometimes thrive regardless, the presence of a good, loving, and active father (preferably a biological father) dramatically increases the best chances of good outcomes for children.

Sometimes, the damage can be less — but the damage may also be total. Children need their fathers.

An effective plan to mitigate damage to one's children should be set up. But is an "effective" plan always possible?

Is there a way to father one's children remotely? Daily positive phone calls to children (and his wife/their mother) to hear how their day was and to offer support, encouragement, and — as possible — help, can maintain a healthy connection with an absent father. However, in some of the situations mentioned above, this may not be easy at all.

Here are some resources to consider: other successful fathers, social workers, even adult children of other families who had to go through the same thing and came out healthy at the other end. Look for help in books. As time and proximity allows, join parenting groups. Consult professionals when necessary. But be aware that, from a child's perspective growing up, *reasons don't matter*. The absence of a father does. The truths of life are sometimes very tough.

Often, fathers themselves need help and support. They

shouldn't try to do it all by themselves, especially when their lives seem overcome by events out of their control.

The same thing happens to mothers, too.

All of us need help at times. But because parents can get over-whelmed with their own lives, many don't realize it. So they don't get any help at all.

Chapter 16

Mental Illness

Before beginning, let me put mental illness in perspective regarding school and other killings by quoting someone who should know about this.

In an interview of April 14, 2023, Dr. Daniel Bober, a psychiatrist and Chief Medical Officer at Odyssey Behavioral Healthcare, was clear:

> *"Mental illness is not the reason for school shootings. Only 4% of interpersonal violence is directly attributable to mental illness."*

Just four percent. Even if two or three times that number, mental illness does not come near to the consistency of fatherlessness, as observed and defined in this book, among school shooters, serial killers, and gang murderers. It does not come close to what the damage of fatherlessness and dysfunctional families appear to be causing.

Therefore, although mental illness truly is a serious problem, based on current data, observers should not assume that it is the primary cause of the killings we have considered here. Nonetheless, it needs to be addressed.

Dr. Bober then went on to express concern about the gun issue in America.

✳✳✳

Our effort should always be to strengthen the foundation of children's lives as they grow up. We need to eliminate or substantively mitigate that which has damaged so many children to the point where others continue to die. Even though commonsense dictates that this must be fixed, it doesn't look like it's happening.

As we have just seen, current evidence of genetic links to mental illness does not appear to be a main issue in these killings, although it has clearly been a factor in some of them.

Nonetheless, with or without a genetic link to it, mental illness is a serious issue. By itself, it can have deadly consequences. Combined with other serious issues, such as fatherlessness, it is even more likely to contribute to violence and deaths.

The Las Vegas shooter was the son of a psychopath and, according to *From a Taller Tower*, may have been a psychopath himself. In some other killers, we might learn of what might be actual or undiagnosed mental illnesses in their families. Nonetheless, it does not appear to be an issue in the majority of involved families.

Observant and concerned parents should take early and effective action and interventions when they see behaviors in their children that normal parenting (however that is defined) is unable to resolve.

Left unattended, it can eventually be too late. Parents may wrongly assume that all will be resolved on its own. (Sometimes, it is.)

Parents will then admit to shock should their child engage in crime or killings that they never saw coming — but should have.

On the other hand, parents can become paranoid about their children's behavior. They can go to the other extreme wrongly assuming that normal childhood behaviors and development are somehow precursors to terrifying violence and death at the hands of their children. A balance is needed, although it can be hard to know what that balance is. That's part of the challenge of parenting.

Nor, however, should parents assume that their children will just grow out of potentially serious behavior, whether or not mental illness might be the cause. Not only may they not grow out of it, but they can get much worse. Many children know how to keep things away from their parents who may already be failing to monitor their children adequately. Parents of school shooters often knew nothing until it was too late.

Having two parents together makes any awareness of abnormal behaviors or possible symptoms of mental illness more likely. A single parent can become overwhelmed with life. Such a parent might not have enough energy or awareness to recognize potential symptoms of mental illness. Even if they see it, they might think that it might somehow be a result of the limited time and resources they have for their children — and not actually a mental health issue at all.

Sometimes, a single parent can be concerned that they might just be paranoid about their child's behavior. Having the other parent around might bring a better perspective. They can talk about any concerns together.

By paying attention to what is going on with their children, strong and competent fathering (and mothering) is potentially capable of preventing, mitigating, or simply identifying when help might be needed for potential mental health issues — as well as for other serious, secretive behavior issues.

Saying that fatherlessness is a major issue is not to say that mental illness is not a serious problem at times.

However, data appear to show a higher percentage of children with serious mental illnesses among those who are fatherless. That alone should put the constant blame on mental illness — which is a problem — back and potentially affected by the foundational issue of fatherlessness.

Among a number of others, Seung-Hui Cho, the 2007 Virginia Tech shooter who killed 32 people and wounded 17 others, was reportedly severely afflicted with mental illness.

Children with unusual, potentially destructive thoughts and behaviors should be quickly evaluated by a professional, more than once if things aren't resolved. Regardless of the cause, closely involved parenting and fathering can and should be able to identify such anomalies and find help. Yet, even when serious behaviors or expressed thoughts indicate the possible presence of illness or serious malbehaviors, many parents remain in denial and do not consider help.

Unfortunately, America currently has a very weak mental illness treatment system. Some people can put off getting help for fear of the costs. Society must not put roadblocks in the way of mentally ill children — and adults — getting expeditious help.

Beyond that, little infrastructure remains of the country's former mental hospital system. Many felt the mentally ill weren't being treated correctly in that system. Indeed, abuses existed. But rather than fixing problems in the system, people chose to dismantle it entirely. It has now become difficult or impossible to get even severely mentally ill people the substantive help that they, and the rest of the country, need.

What we are doing now, especially for those with serious mental illnesses, just isn't working. Many are now homeless.

Drugs also link to mental illness behaviors and crime. Killers often have drug use in their backgrounds. So do some parents.

Rebuilding mental health treatment and support facilities is a major undertaking. Many would continue to oppose it. But, if we want to reduce violence, suicides, and other dangers related to serious mental illnesses, that is what should be done.

Therefore, complaints about mental illness among killers is

worthless unless there is also a strong push to reestablish substantive facilities to treat those who need such help and protection. Nonetheless, even those with mental illness can have the added complication of fatherlessness. Both together can be especially deadly.

Sometimes, one or both parents may have grown up with mental health problems in their families, or in themselves, and don't see these issues as problematic in their children — or they just want to hide their presence.

Many, many people suffer from some level of mental illness, yet most people function (mostly) well, even happily, in the world. Some aren't even diagnosed as having mental illness. Sometimes, it's only when some disturbing incident occurs, especially one of significant violence, that anyone is actually evaluated as to whether they have some kind of mental illness.

Mental illness may be present early in life, or it might show up later on. If not noticed or addressed, its end product can be violence and death, including suicides. Lesser manifestations can lead to sadness, frustration, and hopelessness in the lives of those affected. Why are we not providing enough help?

It's certainly likely that the large increase in the use of prescription drugs being prescribed for various behavioral disorders is also having an effect on the behaviors and emotional health of killers today.

On the other hand, there are indeed times when some people simply become bad, even evil people. They weren't like that when they were born, were they? Something moved them there.

Nonetheless, the clearest, most widespread issue connecting most people of violence — both children and adults — appears to be fatherlessness.

***

Note that although I have experience in many areas of life, I am not a mental health professional. If you feel you might have a need for one, contact an actual professional. Don't wait.

Chapter 17

More Comments About Guns

Reviewing the categories of killers in Chapter Two, we find that focusing exclusively on guns as a foundational cause of deaths is short-sighted.

Guns are just one tool of violence. There are other tools, too. The concern here is about violence *of all sorts and at all levels —* not simply "gun violence." Constant talk about guns ensures that other forms of deadly violence, overwhelmingly also caused by fatherlessness, will be ignored by those with no interest in anything beyond that one issue of guns. It ensures fatherlessness itself will be relegated to the trash heap of disinterest and denial.

Some authors, commentators, and politicians appear to put guns forward as the foundational cause of violence. Many others feel the same way.

In reality, guns are a *tool* of violence, not the cause.

I do not fault those who write about this issue because, in many cases, it is a deeply emotional issue for them. In other cases, it merely seems to be political.

However, I do fault those who appear to place the blame for the many deaths we see nearly entirely on guns (and sometimes also on mental illness).

I find myself stunned by such writers, commentators, and politicians by the near total neglect of what even a cursory review of both recent and past mass killers shows. It is a failure to consider those who have been the *real* mass killers of history, including those who have killed *millions* of people over the past centuries.

Such writings appear to point to what are the only things many want to discuss — and blame — for mass shootings today: mental illness, bullying, a desire for fame, importance, or revenge.

However, many almost exclusively blame the violence and killings on the type, as well as the massive numbers of uncontrolled, available guns. Those can be things of concern. But we must remember that mass killings have not just been seen in recent times, but much earlier, even in ancient times — when guns did not even exist.

***

Guns are regularly used among school shooters and by "common" murderers,[1] including in gang killings. Although killers in other categories may also use guns, many others do not.

Therefore, unless people intentionally choose to disregard whole categories of killings, including the largest ones, they cannot make the case that guns alone are a primary *cause* of killings.

Focusing on guns as a significant cause of these deaths, thinking that, if we can just get rid of them, deaths would plummet, has little support in fact.

Although guns have been used and continue to be used, the vast majority of deaths among children, but also adults over the centuries — taking into account all deaths mentioned in Chapters Two and Seven — were not from guns.

Can we get rid of guns? Estimates are that there are more guns in America than people. From a practical perspective, does anyone think they can all be taken away? Not a chance.

Even if the government actually could take guns away from all cooperative citizens, many others would hide their guns and keep them anyway. Most importantly, criminals wouldn't give up their guns. They are, after all, bad people.

Even if most people were to give up guns as demanded by some, criminal cartels would simply bring in guns from other countries. Because the "good people" are then unarmed, criminals would have free reign. In some places, that's happening today.[2]

Since vast numbers of deaths are from handguns — and knives — why do so many people focus on vaguely-defined "assault weapons?" Do they think banning a single category of weapon — even if possible — would save most of these lives? (They do, but they shouldn't.)

Killers would either get such weapons from other sources, regardless of any ban or, as likely, just find another way to kill people. Remember, when looking at ways the largest numbers of killings occurred, the misnamed "assault weapons" were often not present at all.

Remember that not all fatherless sons in this book used guns to kill their victims. They also employed other methods, partially including starvation, torture, knives, and personal strangulation. So, weapons weren't necessarily the problem; fatherlessness was. (Yes, I know it's more complicated than that.)

Even on its surface, it begins to look pretty convincing that children (later on, even adults) who travel a road to evil and death often did not have a good and involved father in their lives as they grew to adulthood. Many times, that road included their own deaths.

***

Forgive me, once again, as I digress for an extended moment.

This author has definite opinions on what should be done to reduce deaths and promote safer gun ownership fully outside the issue of fatherlessness. That especially includes mandatory firearm training and/or testing, as is done when issuing drivers licenses.

Having served in two branches of the military, I assure you that guns are safer for both the user and those around the user when the gun owner has been through training. Likewise, guns are more effective and can be kept more safely, when someone knows how to correctly use them. Training does that.

US Army trainers don't just hand guns to new recruits and expect them to use them safely and effectively in battle. They are given extensive training and repeated practice, often with multiple kinds of firearms. Not just new recruits, but even fully-trained soldiers, have to pass periodic tests on the firing range to demonstrate that they continue to be proficient when using them.

If the military knows the critical value of training in firearms, why do people in the general public somehow think they'll be able to use them correctly, safely, and effectively (meaning they can hit what they're aiming at) without adequate training?

"Adequate" doesn't mean an hour of familiarization, although that's certainly better than what most people get now. It means multiple lessons under a qualified instructor including actual practice with their firearm. It especially includes firearm safety instruction.

Why do some insist that no one should be "forced" to get training when it actually makes everyone far safer and more effective with their firearms? Too many people are injured or killed in firearm accidents, especially when the firearm owner hasn't completed an adequate (or *any*) training course, and the guided practice that goes with it.[3]

Some states do require varying amounts of firearm training. I continue to hope that such training will be more widely required. One can point to numerous restrictions on *all* rights under the Bill of Rights. I'm not listing examples for each one here, but all should be aware that our enumerated rights are not unlimited, although many assume, or wish, that they were.

In at least one jurisdiction, I'll mention a prohibition that had been put on more than two people gathering together on the streets, even if peaceably. That would clearly seem to violate Freedom of Assembly in the First Amendment. The restriction was put in place as a tool to help control dangerous gang activity, an understandable purpose. A court reviewed it at the time it was introduced and let it remain in place.

Each right has corresponding responsibilities and restrictions. But the right itself remains protected. It's all a delicate balancing act.

The Second Amendment contains the only right that deals with a mechanical device. When it was passed, most people knew how to safely and responsibly use the variety of these mechanical devices that were available to them at the time. But that is not the case today.

A knowledge of the safe and effective workings of that mechanical device really only complements the right to keep and carry it. It doesn't restrict it.

Perhaps the Founding Fathers might have addressed this shortcoming when they wrote the amendment if they had anticipated that people would one day know nothing about them. (Of course, people have also said that about other amendments and various sections of the Constitution.) The Founding Fathers likely made the assumption that people would continue to competently and safely use these devices.

As do others, I like to compare this with driving. What would happen if new drivers were no longer "forced" to get training and pass tests so that we knew they could drive safely? (Even then, we're not always sure though, are we?) I wouldn't want to be on those roads! Of course, driving is not (yet) a constitutional right. Gun ownership is.

I will add that there are extremists on both sides of the gun issue. Some want to get rid of all guns or restrict them such that guns become as rare as talking rabbits. On the other side are those who feel that gun ownership should *never* be restricted at all. Those who support that position haven't really thought that through. Even strong gun advocates support some restrictions.

The military itself has strong restrictions for service members regarding guns used in the military. In reality, there have always been restrictions on gun ownership. When was the last time your five-year-old went in to purchase a couple of firearms to play with on his own?

So the question isn't whether there should be restrictions — there will always be restrictions — but how restrictive they should be.

Just in part, my view is that those with serious mental illnesses, as one example, should not be able to have a gun.

However, background checks can fail to screen out those who should not have guns. Because reports of those with mental illnesses are often not made by other agencies to those doing such checks, those with mental illnesses can continue to obtain guns when they should not. Those with a background of drug abuse can sometimes simply lie on applications and be issued guns anyway. Recently, a famous example of that occurred. Nonetheless, even years later, nothing had been done. We are still waiting to see what might happen there.

I believe that gang members and other dangerous people should not be able to have firearms — although they'll get them illegally anyway. Strong and consistent efforts to stop bad and evil people from getting guns should be made, even though, too often, those efforts will fail.

I support red flag laws with commonsense protections from abusers of the law. However, such protections should not unduly delay quick action when necessary.

There needs to be a balance of commonsense protections among people on both sides of the gun issue.

A fuller discussion of this is for another time.

Although some might suggest otherwise, this digression does not deal with damage of fatherlessness.

We'll move on.

---

1. The term "common" murderers does not mean killings of lesser importance. The term is used to differentiate day-to-day city crime from the killings of larger numbers of people is previously listed in this book. Many times, such killings can include gang murders.
2. To be clear, I support strong laws to deter and punish dangerous criminals, including those committing serious gun crimes. As I write, there have been too many district attorneys in the country who appear to believe the opposite of that.
3. If it were to become an issue, there are ways that training can be designed without leaving a record of people attending after they complete their training.

Chapter 18

School Interventions?

For our purposes, an "intervention" is action taken to get or provide direct help or support to a student or other person felt to pose a danger to others or to himself, in order to eliminate or greatly mitigate such dangers. Schools are rarely good at handling seriously dangerous students themselves. Some special education teachers can be helpful, but not always.

However, schools do often provide *warnings* and pass on serious concerns about potential dangers to parents and staff at the school. They can also notify local child or social services agencies to request special help.

By itself, providing warnings do not stop something bad that might be coming. Taking *action* on such warnings can do that. Unfortunately, some parents not only disregard such warnings, they can become angry with the teacher or school for daring to suggest something might be wrong with their child. Some have insisted on removing their (potentially dangerous) child from such teachers' classes, or even from the school. If a parent gets a warning, they should take it seriously and act on it.

Teachers and administrators are not always right, but their concerns should be taken seriously anyway — and acted upon.

Perhaps it turns out to be nothing of concern. Perhaps a full explanation can put the issue to rest.

Or perhaps that child is ready to embark on something terrible about which the child's parents know nothing. Parents should be serious about looking into all warnings or concerns about behavior issues seen at the school.

In serious cases, most schools will normally take action to try to address what can be potentially deadly situations, but not always. They can't know what's going on with all their students all the time.

Students who can be a danger to themselves — suicides are too common today — as well as a danger to others, need to be found out. Because schools themselves rarely have professional resources onsite to address such problems, schools must get help from outside resources for such students.

Sadly, even in what might be felt to be critical situations by the school, outside resources might be "too busy" to show up to handle even a serious school concern. Most social or behavioral support services are short-handed for all the needs in the community.

Others sometimes seem as though they're just not making serious school needs the priority that such situations should be.

As with so many others, social or behavioral support professionals are often fighting burnout themselves. Who's around to help *them*?

Critical help may not come until the next day — or even the following week. I have personally witnessed this. In some cases, especially outside of larger urban areas, there may be no alternative ways to get help. Those outside the school may not understand the seriousness of a situation. Sometimes, even if they want to help, for one reason or another they can't.

Those living in large urban centers can't understand why smaller communities don't have the greater number of resources that they have — even though some urban centers don't always have enough for their needs either.

Surprising to many who make broad assumptions and

pronouncements about this, some small community schools might not have any substantive medical care facility, mental health resources, or even trained police readily available in their communities at all.

The bottom line is that schools themselves are not equipped for actual interventions. They may not always be able to easily refer students or potentially serious problems to outside agencies. Nonetheless, outsiders can wrongly blame schools for not taking action.

Schools aren't normally trained to diagnose something wrong with a student except by happenstance, by noticing troublesome behaviors. Schools weren't designed to provide that kind of support.

Schools are for instruction and staff are there to *teach*. Schools might notice potential signs of trouble, and some might be able to intervene, but that is not their primary role.

Even though educating students is their main purpose, that isn't always done well either.

For more on this, see the book, *Education Is Dead,* by the author.

Nonetheless, teachers, counselors, and administrators often do call parents with concerns and warnings about their children. Too many times, some parents do not follow up, even if they take the school report seriously in the first place.

Even in potentially serious cases, law enforcement may not want to, or be legally able to get involved unless evidence of a crime is present or serious evidence of one about to be committed comes to light. Sometimes, law enforcement personnel will help with other things, but that often depends on their local department, its officers, and their available time.

Teachers and other school personnel often correctly sense that something is seriously wrong, but do not (yet) have actual "evidence" satisfactory for police. Even behavioral services sometimes require evidence that is not readily available before behavioral professionals will come to look into it.

Nonetheless, both police and behavioral professionals should take school concerns seriously and move to offer what help they can — they should at least try to fully *evaluate* a concern — before something actually happens.

Once again, parents need to take warnings and concerns from schools seriously. Those might be the only alerts they will have.

There are strong suggestions from mental health and social services professionals, as well as the general public, that schools need to hire additional resource officers or mental health professionals. Those making such recommendations don't fully understand the limited resources available to most schools.

Many schools, especially smaller ones, have budgets that can barely keep their foundational educational programs running. They often need more teachers and staff just to fulfill their main task of educating — or trying to educate — their students.

Countless schools don't have school counselors, nurses, or other support staff, although they would be very helpful if they had additional staff. But who will pay for them? Usually no one. Both schools and school districts themselves are often short of money.

All that assumes such staff would even be available to hire. There is a shortage of specialized staff in many of these areas.

Many such specialized staff would end up being asked to do double-duty when other staff aren't available, even if it's outside their original hiring responsibilities. Schools should have the flexibility to temporarily assign such staff to help out in whatever way would be in the best interests of students and the school.

With background as a professional educator, I cannot object to that.

The bottom line here is that schools often can't provide whichever "interventions" those outside the school think it's their job to provide. Even if schools have the funding, it just isn't their job. Education is. Nonetheless, it is important for schools to be involved with this issue. Lives can be at stake. So can the futures of the children, and the country.

With limited exceptions — in special education, for example — they're not fully trained for it. Nor do staff at school have time to go around evaluating the mental state of every student every day.

This is not to say that school should not take care of their students outside their tasking of educating them. They certainly should and they do.

But it's important that parents pay special attention to warnings or notices of behavioral issues in their children from the school. They need to evaluate their own children through daily talking, good parenting, and oversight. Involved fathers should be an important part of this.

Chapter 19

*What To Do About Absent Fathers

This is the final section adapted from:
THE CARTAINOS
MEN OF PASSION • MEN OF STONE.

T he issue of absent fathers is mentioned often today, but the conversation quickly moves on to other things. After all, what can we do about it?

Recall that David Blankenship called this *"Our Most Urgent Social Problem."* And it is. But nothing effective is being done to address it.

A large number of our most critical social problems can be traced back to this single issue. Poverty, crime, abortion, addictions, homelessness, mental health issues, sexually transmitted diseases, and more can all have roots in fatherlessness.

Today people and governments try to address those symptoms, but not their primary cause. In spite of data, there is not even an acceptance that absent fathers and low-quality fathering is a foundational cause at all.

At the time of this writing, student debt is destroying the lives of an enormous number of people. Instead of developing as confident, independent adults — and, therefore, good fathers — many "children" remain living home long after having finished their schooling. High housing costs are contributing to this unhealthy trend.[1]

Some children — who are no longer children — become overwhelmed. Others become far too comfortable living their lives with their parents.

And what about children who have no parents? Perhaps their parents died, can barely afford to support themselves, or are otherwise unable or unwilling to let their children stay with them.

Then what about older foster children who may be forced to make their own way in the world? Who is there to help these now-adult children? These are new adults, just out of school — or perhaps still in school — but without the resources to enter the world.

Of course, some children, who choose a non-college path in life may find a way to become independent well before others who complete college. In some cases, they may even become employers of those later college graduates.

But nothing is simple. Research shows that other issues also affect families and children. But absent and low-quality fathering should become front and center.

Most people lack full and accurate information about the critical need for fathers. Even before 12th grade, schools should begin providing unbiased education regarding the essential nature of fathers. Sadly, some students would have already become biological parents by then.

Can unbiased education about this even exist? Doubtful. Again, I recommend the book, *Education Is Dead,* by the author.

Another option is to provide parents with the information they need to help them personally provide some structured education about the importance of fathers and families to their own children. Parents might also provide children with their own independent guidance, too.

The problem here is that many parents would not be comfortable doing that kind of thing. Or they might assume their wonderful children would never do the wrong thing in the first place. Tough choices here.

There should be a nationwide campaign to get out the information and research about the crisis of absent fathers — and the results of their absence. But none of that is enough. Regardless, the problem must be clearly and effectively addressed head-on.

Here are five suggestions for a broader discussion to address the issue. However, additional plans and support must also be put into place. The problem is massive. The solutions must be massive, too.

(1) In order to keep fathers with their children, marriage itself must be strengthened so that both parents stay together with their children. Research is clear as to the importance of marriage related to this issue. Marriage support should include easily accessible counseling in advance of marriage, but especially practical support and help during the marriage itself. The goal is to keep marriages together so that fathers can stay closely involved in the lives of their children.

Husbands and fathers must feel supported and comfortable at home with their wives. Of course, absent issues of abuse, for example, wives and mothers must also feel comfortable. I again refer you to Linda Waite's recommended book, *The Case for Marriage*. There are many books and resources on this.

(2) Laws and court procedures and decisions must be re-examined. Changes must be undertaken to eliminate traditional biases against fathers especially related to custody and visitation arrangements. They are less common today but, in far too many places, this is still a serious problem.

A June 21, 2020, article by Jack Brewer talked about the serious issues impacting fathers. It then added:

To make matters worse, many fathers like myself who actually want to be full-time dads are held back by archaic child custody and child support legislation which systematically opposes granting equal parenting opportunity to willing fathers.[2]

(3) Even when biological fathers have left home, there should be a personal outreach to each absent father. As possible, provisions must be made so that good fathers are able to provide quality fathering for their children. Minimally, fathers and their children should spend substantively more time together.

As we know, statistics on fatherlessness differ. But, regardless of precise numbers, all of the data is terrible. That earlier June 2020 article by Jack Brewer quoted statistics that *"73 percent of African-American kids [are] born out of wedlock."* It also said that *"71 percent of American high school dropouts are fatherless."* It noted that a child without a father [most often a son] is *20 times more likely to end up in prison.*

To bring society back to health, good and involved fathers are needed by their children. Although not always possible, the best way to handle that is to keep families intact.

We also can't forget that many men remain very good fathers for their children even after a separation or divorce — or at least as much as possible. Supportive mothers often contribute to those successes. It is not those fathers with whom we are concerned.

If this problem is approached by placing blame on fathers, it will fail. The approach must be as neutral as practical and supportive of all involved consistent with accomplishing the goal. There must also be an understanding that the issue exists beyond just children and their fathers.

Emotions surrounding a former marriage are often so sensitive that any poorly thought out interactions can torpedo efforts to get fathers back with their children.

Relationships between mothers and fathers are not always bad. One must take into account that many fathers (and mothers) are still attached to the other person — still in love with them. Contact, or a mere remembrance of their previous connection, may remain painful to some because of that continuing love. Other times, bitterness or anger must be managed.

All this must be taken into account in trying to pull fathers and their children together. Whether or not fathers and mothers seem amenable to such efforts, children usually are (assuming mothers have not irrevocably undermined their fathers).

Yet, even when children appear angry or frustrated about their fathers, a sensitive, substantive, and positive increase in contact is almost always beneficial. As possible, this should be done regardless of the ages of the children. With a proper attitude, combined with supportive preparation between parents, even much older children might benefit — even as children become adults.

Outreach to fathers should be separate from any child support issues. Children need their fathers in ways that are entirely separate from financial support, even though that is important, too.

Although some readers will disagree, the financial support of children is indeed separate from providing good fathering to children. It is important, but men who have to pay for children without a corresponding healthy relationship with them, may become even more bitter than they may have already been.

Being a real father is not merely defined as providing money to people he never sees and who may not even care about him — except as a source of money. This has been an ongoing issue as long as fathers have helped to financially support their children.

Allowing this one issue to keep fathers out of their children's lives is generally counterproductive. As fathers, acting as fathers, spend more time together with their children, some issues of financial support have a greater chance of being smoothed out anyway. However, as appropriate, continuing serious issues involving financial support should be referred elsewhere.

(4) Bringing God back to families is a positive thing. Data often support that. Many church and social programs have seen success in what some feel are significant numbers. Unfortunately, it's only by comparison. Such programs have not been nearly pervasive enough to handle the enormity of the problem throughout society. We must do far better than we are doing now.

(5) Strong, successful fathers, even if their children are grown and away, should mentor other men.

✳✳✳

Providing adequate and widespread support for families, with targeted efforts to bring fathers back with their children, will require a massive number of caring people trained to be sensitive and knowledgeable of the issues. Outreach to fathers requires actual people reaching out to them through supportive calls and personal visits.

Such a massive mobilization would only be possible by establishing yet another level of bureaucracy.

Many people bristle at that thought. I can't disagree with such concerns. But have other options worked? They have not. The problem is worse than ever.

There are currently various United States cabinet departments that address other vital issues for countless Americans. These departments cannot handle everything, but they can make a significant difference nonetheless.

These include problems of adequate housing for those unable to fully afford their own — the Department of Housing and Urban Development: HUD. Addressing issues of various aspects of health throughout America is the Department of Health and Human Services: HHS.

The Administration of Children and Families (ACF) exists within the Department of Health and Human Services (HHS).[3] It purportedly *"promotes the economic and social well-being of families, children, individuals, and communities."*

Most people don't even know it exists.

Nor does their praiseworthy outreach site, fatherhood.gov, reach enough people to effect changes.

To address the issue of fatherlessness, both the ACF and fatherhood.gov are inadequate. At least on the surface, the ACF does not appear to put "fatherlessness" front and center among its several programs. Yet the problem of absent fathers is well known.

Might we simply add or augment support for addressing fatherlessness within the ACF? It does not appear to have the resources necessary to make sufficient inroads to address this national crisis. To an outsider, the mere existence of father issues can seem missing, or perhaps buried among its many other goals. That is not good enough.

A new and separate cabinet-level department should be considered in order to more aggressively address this issue.

Whatever programs the government might currently have in place to address this problem — if any — have failed.

Unlike too many current departments, the people of America must know that a new Department of Family and Father Support actually exists — and what it does. Otherwise, those who need it won't use it.

In addition, we can't wait for fathers to search for and use available services, even if they might be adequate — and few are. We must go directly to fathers themselves.

Establishing a Department of Family and Father Support (DFFS) would be a logical step in addressing this issue.

Those who complain that it appears to leave out mothers — it doesn't — are clearly unfamiliar with the data and damage related to fatherlessness. The new department is not here to make people "feel good" or "equitable." It's here to address a specific and very serious problem.

Immediately after this new department's establishment, steps must be taken so that the American people widely understand the pervasiveness and damage caused by fatherlessness. People must then understand the resources available to combat it.

It might pattern itself on that of the stop-smoking campaigns of decades past. In that instance, a widespread campaign in all media was undertaken. Its frequent public service announcements continued for years. The extensive campaign strongly and repeatedly encouraged people to stop smoking. It was all but impossible for anyone to miss its messages. It was effective in getting its message out.

In that and in other ways, the full extent of the problem of fatherlessness can be regularly brought before the public. Such a nationwide campaign is absolutely needed, including in schools and in local and national media. Only then, will a new DFFS be able to take action to address this problem that is, by then, supported by more of the population.

However, the messages by themselves are not enough. Concurrent actions must include one-on-one outreach and support for fathers and families. The current system of social services supporting a family is not enough to address this new, targeted program. After all, *nothing has worked until now,* and that includes, as good and essential as they are, the outreach of sometimes overwhelmed (other times, underutilized) non-profits, churches, and social workers.

An aggressive action plan with funding for the significant number of people needed to provide such services must be put together.

Plenty of people oppose any proposal for yet another government program — simply because it is yet another government program. That is completely understandable.

Really, few of us should want another government program. But, here, no other entity has the resources of the government to address the massive extent of this problem across an entire nation.

Even a Department of Family and Father Support (DFFS) would be inadequate to handle the full problem. That is the same for HUD, HHS, and other government departments.

None can solve all problems for all the people within their tasking. But they all can make progress, sometimes substantial progress.

A national DFFS program can set standards of service that may help states and other entities to add in their own complementary plans.

***

"But I don't want another government program!"

"I understand. So, what do you suggest that will address the problem effectively?"

"I don't know, but it's not that!"

And so the problem continues.

***

Although issues of financial support can certainly be brought up as appropriate, the role of a Department of Family and Father Support should not be for legal enforcement activities. Other entities should handle that separately.

Anything that does not directly support children having an actual father who is positively involved in their lives perpetuates the problem rather than helps to solve it.

Nor should its purpose be to promote or enforce whichever politically correct view of fatherhood or parenting might be in fashion. These are sure ways to keep families broken and fathers away from their children.

Let me repeat that admonition: The purpose of *any* such program must not be to enforce or encourage specific fathering or parenting methods presented by way of any specific political or sociologically-based thinking. In most cases, that is *regardless* of purportedly "proven" evidence of one way or another way to parent. Such specific guidance in a particular direction that takes the authority out of the hands of parents should be anathema [repugnant and unacceptable].

However, that does not preclude teaching and helping to protect from certain obvious things that may be damaging or ineffective and about which there would be near universal agreement.

That is likely the most sensitive part of doing this.

With other protections, privacy should be strongly built into its work. Otherwise, there will not be the open communication necessary among the parties. In some cases, privacy can also ensure personal safety.

Nothing is easy. But *doing nothing,* as is happening now, can't be acceptable either. This is indeed a national crisis — and not just in America.

Supporting and working with various church and secular programs that have shown continued success should be part of the recommended resources within DFFS. There is much to be learned from those more limited programs. If appropriate and agreeable, such programs can be incorporated into DFFS — even if run independently.

The work of the Department of Family and Father Support must be far broader than anything currently available.

If this is as underfunded as other departments, it will fail. This is an urgent issue and it must be treated that way.

Fathers should see people from DFFS as supportive, caring, and respectful of them *as fathers.* Its primary effort should be to keep families together and to bring absent fathers regularly together with their children. It should also provide resources to strengthen marriage itself.

Although she does not address the issue of missing fathers directly, Linda Waite's book contains several worthy proposals for supporting healthy families. Those should be reviewed and, as possible, implemented.

Separately from what is here, organizations like The Woodson Center, founded by Bob Woodson in 1981, have looked at the issue of fatherlessness in Black families from a historical perspective. They force us to move away from the unhelpful rhetoric and damaging programs of recent generations. They can give us a new place from which to begin.

Their work also suggests practical methods and goals that are not considered in most public and private programs today. Ways of working to solve fatherlessness can often be applied to all people and all races.

But, whatever is done will require a national commitment to address the situation. The issue affects all races and all economic classes throughout the country.

***

Although this is a call for action, that call and these proposals are massive undertakings. Further, I am a realist. The likelihood that any of this will happen is pretty slim.

Nonetheless, there may be no other way to turn around the continuing and increasing harm done to people and society as a result of absent fathers and disrupted families.

Absent some miracle, I recognize it will not happen except as a strongly bipartisan undertaking. As has often happened, the personal agendas of those involved can torpedo the entire effort.

Do I feel optimism and hope that this problem can be overcome? I do not. But the alarm must be sounded. We must all enter the battle. If we do, we might be able to turn this around.

What we should not accept is this common refrain in response to hearing of some new government program — or any program: *"I don't know what the answer is, but it's not that!"*

We cannot allow that response to stand. It will only ensure that nothing will continue to happen. If someone has an actual workable and nationwide solution, then put it on the table. Otherwise, don't refuse to consider anything and everything that even makes an attempt to address the problem.

Even though none of us should want another government program, sometimes, out of necessity, it's all we've got.

All people should be angry, even frightened, about the current situation. Leaders who rise up must undertake this as the national and global problem that it is. Unless countless courageous people rise to fight against the loss of fatherhood, we may indeed, as Popenoe warns, "*...be on the verge of committing social suicide.*"

Who we are now, what the world's countries are now, what remaining values we all still purport to hold — much of that upon which our society was founded — will be gone. None of this is a healthy thing, nor should it be accepted as part of what many wrongly see as normal, evolving changes in society.

The screaming, unseen damage due to fatherlessness is so destructive that support for Popenoe's warning would seem to be before us.

There are no miraculous answers to the problems we face. But finding help for the problem of absent fathers and failing families can genuinely help to address a vast number of our societal ills today.

Perhaps a serious discussion of the thoughts presented here could be a starting point.

---

1. *See, for example: fortune.com/2022/03/25/more-adults-living-with-parents-than-ever-pew-research-pandemic-covid-great-depression, accessed 2-19-2023.*

2. *From an opinion piece by Jack Brewer entitled,* This Father's Day, let's also remember the fatherless: Former NFL Safety Jack Brewer *published June 21, 2020 (Father's Day) at Fox Business.com.*

3. *Website: acf.hhs.gov. Accessed Oct. 5, 2019.*

Chapter 20

Once More: What Can Be Done?

As just suggested, a massive national effort is needed to address this problem. The vast numbers of fathers and families needing support would likely be on a scale never seen before.

When dealing with an effort of this size, our options are limited. Any program must be at no cost to fathers and families.

Let's start by looking at four things that have little chance to work nationally, but can still offer local or regional help.

(1) Putting the responsibility *exclusively* on private, non-profit, or government-supported organizations.

These groups are too small. It is uncertain how well they can work cooperatively with other programs or the government. Although some can be very positive, many can be philosophically biased to such a degree as to be unacceptable to many fathers and families. That is actually a significant problem in all entities, public or private.

That doesn't mean that these organizations should not be

involved. Some are indeed very effective and this problem needs all the help it can get.

(2) Social Services professionals or entities.

Generally too small and underfunded. Then, too, they are often philosophically biased to such a degree that they, too, can be unacceptable to many fathers and families. Although a design to work together with multi-sided control, coordination, and philosophies might be possible, it would be a new design. It would be a delicate balancing act. Of course, this would be true elsewhere, too. Without a radical redesign, substantial funding, and a massive enlisting of personnel, this may not succeed. These professionals and entities are generally overwhelmed even without the addition of a major new program. Nonetheless, we need to harness as many resources as we can.

(3) Churches and religious groups.

Even working with each other, they are also too small and underfunded for a national effort. They, too, would need government funding. However, they may have a greater breadth of philosophies consistent with current studies of fathering and parenting. They might show good success and effectiveness, at least for their own communities, if not also beyond. As elsewhere, adequate personnel would not be available for what would be difficult work with the great number of fathers and families who might benefit from what they can offer. Nonetheless, they can and should certainly be involved to address the problem. Some have reportedly been very effective.

(4) Privately Funded efforts.

If several wealthy individuals or foundations joined together, there might be enough funding. However, potentially all can have such strong political, social, or cultural leanings as to make them too biased to function effectively on a widespread basis. Can that be overcome? On paper, it can be. In practice, it's doubtful. Because of the vast number of personnel needed to individually reach out to every father and family in the country who need these services, it is still not likely that even combined funding from multiple well-funded individuals and entities could handle it. Nonetheless, there is a place for any entity that can show positive results in this crisis. This could be one of them.

Are there better options?

(1) We can combine all of the things above and add on whatever we can.

This means bringing all of the above together in one nationally-funded and coordinated effort. But the coordination would be staggering. Those entities should be able to retain their distinctive differences while being flexible enough to function and support diverse people while working with the government and a variety of other organizations. That means that funding must come without the strings of political or sociological agendas — as long as progress is being made towards the goal of massively reducing the number of children with absent or low quality fathers.

Nonetheless, doubts exist regarding their widespread and substantive success. The availability of other options in a community might help provide other choices to fathers and families who need such support.

(2) The Government can cover the country.

As mentioned in the previous chapter, few want another government program. Justifiably, there is great suspicion regarding any new government program. Certain government agencies have recently shown themselves too unusually biased and political-leaning to be trustworthy. Even with massive funding for this, government agencies often use their funding poorly.

Nonetheless, there are advantages to place a program primarily with the government itself. Funding might be more easily allocated. Government entities have experience hiring and coordinating tens of thousands of people. If they have a sense of urgency and good leadership, this may be the most efficient way to gear up and get a nationwide program up and running quickly. Even the first option above, combining numerous nationwide resources, would likely need a government program to coordinate everything. Recall that the previous chapter proposed a new and separate cabinet level department. That is still likely to be the only way to move this forward (relatively) expeditiously.

If there were a nationwide catastrophe, the federal government is expected to step in. This is such a catastrophe. But it is a quiet one. In spite of a widespread acknowledgment of the problem, and even though it is right in front of them, this is still little-seen by most people.

We can stay open to options, but doing nothing should no longer be acceptable. If the federal government doesn't take action, individual states still can. But an effective program comes at great cost. Would states alone have enough?

Other factors contribute to the killings about which this book has been concerned. However, a serious look into the fathering of these killers should be foundational. Beyond that, we should take a fresh look at how to see at-risk situations earlier and try to address them much further in advance.

. . .

***

Regardless of the entity, what people would run such a program? What philosophies would be made part of the support for fathers and dysfunctional families? Any effective program would have to entail one-on-one work, generally with an appropriate male mentor, as well as in-person work with each family. This is an intensive design that would require a large number of people, both paid and volunteer.

These are major problems, but we can't let any possibly effective solutions die if we have any hope of fixing things. Questions must be answered — and quickly. It's unlikely we can answer them all. But we must begin.

As in the past, there will be those who tell us to "follow the science." There have been many past studies on families that are often taught by behavioral and social services professionals and which would undoubtedly be quoted. But we can't fall into a one-size-fits-all approach to this.

It would be difficult to agree on desirable father and family characteristics. Flexibility would have to be a hallmark of any program in working with families.

There are statistics that show that certain characteristics of families show greater success in life than others. Religious entities can correctly point to stronger families when all are involved in religious activities and beliefs. It is good and important to bring God back into the family on a much more widespread basis. However, many on the other side of that would push back strongly in an effort to prevent it.

It's likely there would even be push back by some who want to stop families from voluntarily bringing God and faith into their families. These counterproductive people would point to constitutional issues while, at the same time, ignoring the constitution when unfavorable to their position. If something works —

including God, as just a single example — it should be allowed, though never demanded — as part of the program.

There might be multiple designs available so that fathers and families can choose the one with which they are most comfortable. Other times, a Father and Family Mentor (FFM), part of the new Department of Family and Father Support, might suggest one. If one doesn't seem to be working, they can switch to a different one.

Naturally, Father and Family Mentors must be carefully chosen. They must be well-matched with the fathers and families with whom they will work. If they don't work out, someone else can be found.

Far more would be needed than would be available. Finding enough good and life-experienced people to be Father and Family Mentors would be a major undertaking. We would undoubtedly fall short as the program moves forward.

Pilot programs should be expeditiously implemented to learn what works and what needs adjustment.

What should *not* be done is to force any *governmental, political, or sociological* philosophy onto fathers and families. What some consider to be worthy of banning, others may consider to be perfectly acceptable. Only the most (nearly) universally agreed upon behavioral prohibitions for families should be part of proposed programs.

If an ideology becomes so strong as to alienate one participant or another, that person can leave. But that might effectively end the project for that family. Above all, there must be flexibility and compromise.

Regardless of what is said here, no entity — government or otherwise — should intrude on the sanctity of a father and a family beyond issues of health and safety for both children and parents. The bottom line is to support the growth and development of healthy children. That, in turn, strengthens new families, communities, and the country. The health and happiness of parents is an integral part of that.

Legislation would undoubtedly need to be passed to support

such a wide-ranging program. There would be great suspicion about how any legislative programs would be designed. Lawmakers would push to include their personal philosophies. Even when some insist on supposedly "following the science," it can still lead to serious issues at the family level.

This is all very delicate.

On the other hand, there really *are* issues we know of that generally lead to failures for children within families that cannot be ignored. Yet there will be plenty of people arguing just that — to ignore anything that differs from their own sociological or political philosophies.

This is very hard. Are there no *workable* options to what we have already suggested that might tackle the currently horrendous situation? Do you see options?

The public must have input. However, those who just want to step in and stop it from happening because it doesn't support their personal agenda must be handled carefully. To allow anyone to stop this from moving forward allows the continued destruction of children, families, and the country indefinitely.

Is any of this actually possible? Likely not. I have brought up things to consider. But an actual program would have to be the product of discussions by many people in all walks of (family) life, not just "professionals."

If nothing is done, there will be no change. The foundation of the American family will continue to deteriorate. It's already fallen too far. Children raised in fatherless or dysfunctional families will later pass on those failures to their own families, to their own children. Yet they will assume that all is right and good. After all, that's how they were raised.

Without doing something, fatherless children will be growing up with a serious loss within them, whether they know it or not. Eventually, many will find themselves in old age still hurting, still sad.

Things are a mess.

***

I must warn again that it is the responsibility of *both parents* — if two are available, otherwise the one who is left — to step up and *parent their children*. That means knowing where they are at all times, restricting, as appropriate, where they go and what they do, and closely monitoring their online presence. Both parents and children should understand that it is not the "right" of any child, no matter what age, to have their own cell phones or computers. Where parents permit them, *parents* are responsible for the consistent oversight of their children.

Children should not be abandoned on such devices where they can make their own decisions, often wrong ones. Many parents still know nothing about what they are doing. Children should never be outside the control or — loving, but firm — guidance of parents.

Meet your children's friends. Consider meeting their parents, too.

As possible, do fun and enriching things as a family at least once a week, more often with younger children. Always be talking together. Go to church together.

Social media? It is my personal suggestion that children — and even most adults — are healthier and safer if they do not participate in social media sites. The dangers are real.

There are sometimes legitimate reasons to allow children to venture to social media sites on a limited basis, but the dangers such interactions pose can cause both current and later damage, even when those children become adults. Damage can indeed last a lifetime.

In recent years, there are many real world examples of this.

It is important that children must be brought up carefully with a strong sense of right and wrong, with a strong sense of morality, with a sense of the importance of caring for others. Sadly, these things are often not done today. Too often, that is because such things were never instilled in parents themselves.

. . .

✳✳✳

We must not shrink from these responsibilities. If parents need help or advice, they should ask for it. These things must be brought back now. And addressing the issue of fatherlessness must be done on a national scale.

We either do something now, or we continue to watch what is going on — including the repeated national disaster of more killers killing more people. Too many people will continue to blame what we all see — including murders of all kinds — on issues that have little or nothing to do with fixing the bottom line. Fixing those other issues is rarely even possible.

On the other hand, without a national consensus and support of the people, fixing the foundational issue of fatherlessness might not be either.

Even if, by some magical incantation, all guns throughout the country could disappear, the problem of killers and deaths would continue because the bottom line problem hasn't been fixed: absent, bad, or low-quality fathers and dysfunctional families. Countless lives of frustration and sadness would continue.

Because it's currently unlikely that the country will aggressively go after this problem, schools should then be secured in an effort to protect them from dangerous students, as well as others. However, having a single *unarmed* security officer is not an effective option. In larger schools, having just one security officer, even if armed, might also not be adequate to protect students and staff in an emergency situation.

In front of us all must be the one dominant issue of strong, loving fathers and strong, healthy families. Too many studies, too much evidence, points to this as the foundational problem — and it's getting worse.

If some feel there is not yet enough substantive data in this book, in quoted sources, and in other places, I invite you to do your own studies and research into it. But don't take too much time. More people will have been killed by the time you're done.

Who will make the first move to fix this?

The future depends not only on that first move, but on all the ones after it.

Good luck to us all.

www.ingramcontent.com/pod-product-compliance
Lightning Source LLC
Chambersburg PA
CBHW072012290326
41934CB00007BA/1064